MY LIFE AND HISTORY

BERTA SZEPS

(*from the painting by Carrière*)

MY LIFE AND HISTORY

BY

BERTA SZEPS

(FRAU SZEPS-ZUCKERKANDL)

Translated by
John Sommerfield

CASSELL
AND COMPANY LTD.
LONDON, TORONTO, MELBOURNE
AND SYDNEY

First published 1938

PRINTED IN GREAT BRITAIN
BY NORTHUMBERLAND PRESS LIMITED, GATESHEAD ON TYNE
F.938

To

EMIL ZUCKERKANDL

I DEDICATE

THIS FILM OF MY LIFE

LIST OF ILLUSTRATIONS

INTRODUCTION

THIS book is not just the memoirs of an old lady. First and foremost, because of the brilliant part played by my father in his country's affairs and in international politics, and also through my connections with so many outstanding personalities in European art, politics, and science, my life has been lived behind the scenes of much of the drama of the last sixty years of Europe's history.

So, in this book, I have tried to let my own voice of to-day speak as little as possible. I have used the original documents and letters bequeathed to me by my father—papers that speak with the true voice of history. These I have linked together with extracts from the diary that I have kept ever since I was a child of thirteen. Again, much of this diary is not concerned with my private life, but is a record of personal contact with contemporary artistic and political events.

Before my marriage I acted as a secretary to my father who, through his editorship of the *Neues Wiener Tagblatt*, through his close relationship with the Liberal Crown Prince Rudolf, through his personal connections with the leaders of thought and action in many countries, and above all through his marvellous personality, brought me into contact with people and movements such as few young girls have had the opportunity of knowing.

Above all, these documents and letters and interviews, these extracts from my diary and newspaper articles, deal with the inner history of my own country—with Austria, whose last sixty years of life and whose dreadful fate have been the epitome of all the turmoils, wars, intrigues, sufferings, and splendours of a continent.

7

During the long agony of my country's sufferings in the War, and of its dismemberment afterwards, it was my lot to be placed in a position where I myself became a minor actor in this historic scene. The pages of my diary during these days record diplomatic and political struggles and intrigues during the War and immediately after that have never been made public before.

And now that Austria's drama is over and the darkness has closed upon it, I look back at those bright days of pre-war Vienna, upon all the brilliance and turmoil, all the creative effort of those times, and above everything I remember the kind and wise figure of my father, and wish that his foresight had been acted upon, that Austria had given heed to his prophecy that she would be overwhelmed with darkness unless she allied herself with the Western Democratic Powers.

Since my father and my sister, Sofie Clémenceau, both play such leading roles in the story that I have to tell, I should like to include brief descriptions of them before the story opens.

Moritz Szeps, my father, had a fine, aristocratic face, framed by a black beard; shining blue eyes, eyes which showed his goodness, but which could also flash with anger. It was his eyes that really showed his character. He was a well-proportioned, medium-sized man, with small, nervous hands.

If he had not been a fine writer with a genius for organization, his powers of public speaking would have brought him a tremendous career as a popular orator and political leader. His personality was so fascinating that everybody who came into contact with him was drawn to him as if by some magnetic power. He had studied medicine; but soon his obvious journalistic talents, his brilliant understanding of politics and his power of comprehending all the intricate relationships between contemporary historical events, made him abandon medicine and give all his time to a public career. It was not long before he was in the front rank of European journalists.

8

At the time when he founded the *Neues Wiener Tagblatt*—a democratic newspaper—political journalism was of much more importance than it is to-day. A really first-class editor could have an enormous influence on the bearing of politics, and could as a helper and a leader play a decisive part in the culture and affairs of a nation.

It was the lot of Moritz Szeps to work for Austria, not only within his country, but in Europe generally. His artistic and unconventional nature made him beloved by everybody, especially for what is perhaps the best of all virtues—his sense of humour. A dynamic strength and sanguine nature helped him throughout life, and especially at times when fate seemed against him.

In his view of the future and his political outlook my father was a pessimist, always seeing threatening dangers and complications; but in his actions he was an optimist; and this contradiction within him was destined to be a decisive factor in his life.

My sister Sofie, later the wife of Paul, and sister-in-law of Georges Clémenceau, was one of the best looking and most elegant members of a youthful Viennese society. Behind her cool restraint was hidden a burning enthusiasm for liberty and progress, as if she had foreseen that her life would be fulfilled in Republican France. She moved for half a century amidst an atmosphere of political storm and artistic strife, continuing the tradition of her father's house brilliantly in France, where she was called " La belle Madame Clémenceau ", and was considered to be one of the most elegant women in France.

PART I

CHAPTER I

DIARY

Monday, April 13th, 1878.

My father gave me this diary only yesterday, and to-day something has already happened to me that is quite certainly worth while writing down. My father took me and Sofie to the Liechtenstein picture gallery. I don't know a lot about pictures, but I am certain that I have never seen anything that has impressed me so much as the pictures by Rembrandt. It quite overwhelmed me, and I felt rather relieved when we went down into the garden. There Father pointed to the other side of the road where a house was being built, and he said, " This is where we are going to live after next autumn. I have had the house built for you children. Let's hope and pray that you will all be happy in it."

Then he led us across to see the house. It is really very beautiful; there are only two stories, but it is surrounded by a huge garden. I think it is the loveliest garden I have ever seen. On the ground floor of the house will be bedrooms for Father and Mother, and each of the boys will have a separate bedroom. There will be one for me and one for Sofie, and even one for Ella (the youngest) all to herself except for the governess of course.

On the first floor will be the reception rooms, and there is a heavenly staircase leading up to them. Father has promised me that I will be allowed to be present at the first big reception after we have moved in. So will Sofie, of course, but she will be sixteen by then. . . .

Vienna, October 14th, 1878.

To-day we moved into the new house. It really is simply wonderful! The balustrades of the staircase are made of wrought iron, and on the landing they are of ebony. The best thing is that one can sit at the top and slide all the way down to the bottom in a long curve. Leo and Julius and I did it at once, but of course Sofie wouldn't, she thinks that she is grown up when really she is not much older than I.

We were allowed down to dinner with Father and Mother in the big dining-room. It is the first time we have done this; but I didn't really enjoy it very much. Mother was quite upset, and I think she wanted to cry, because Father said that he had to leave Vienna that night. Mother has to manage all the rest of the moving-in herself now; but Father has to go to Berlin. There is some world congress on there, and it is very important; he said that Mother mustn't be upset at his staying away for a whole month, she really shouldn't think it is a long time when she remembers that they are going to divide up and alter the whole world at this congress.

Berlin, October 25th, 1878.

. . . so Mother didn't want to stay by herself in Vienna for so long, and so she decided to surprise Father in Berlin by just arriving there without saying anything. I must say it is very nice being in our family, Mother had just to ask for the station-master at the (Vienna) North Station and say that she wanted to go to Berlin; and the next morning there was a saloon car at our disposal, which they joined on to the ordinary express.

Not only did Leo and Julius and I go, but we took Wolfi. That was the great advantage of the saloon car, we wouldn't have been allowed to take a dog with us in an ordinary train compartment. He didn't seem to be upset or worried by the journey at all, in fact I think he rather liked it. . . .

Father was staying at a very fine hotel called the "Kaiserhof". He hadn't the faintest idea that we had come to Berlin.

We crept up to the door of his apartment and knocked. I was terribly excited when I heard his voice answer impatiently, "Come in." He was absolutely dumbstruck with astonishment, and it was some time before he said anything. Then he embraced us all and said how pleased he was.

14

There was a man with him, and I was afraid that we might have interrupted them in some private discussion. This man was sitting in an armchair by the table, and he really was extraordinary looking. His appearance reminded me of the pictures of sorcerers that I had imagined for myself when I was little. He stood up, and bowed to Mother, and my father introduced him. Later Mother told us that he was an Englishman, called Disraeli, and was a very famous and important person.

I wasn't pleased to see him, because I was so glad to see Father and it would have been nicer if there were no strangers there. But Mr. Disraeli didn't seem to mind us, I must say. He stroked my hair, and said to Father : " What a charming child." But he soon went and left us alone.

That evening there was a meeting of all the diplomats at the hotel, and Father took us to look at the reception from the balcony. We saw Disraeli again, talking with a very big man, who was so much bigger than he was that poor Disraeli had to take three steps to his one. Mother told us that it was Bismarck. I know about him, and that he is the greatest Chancellor that Germany has ever had, but I still do not like him.

I don't think Berlin is as nice as Vienna, and I am very pleased that we are going home already to-day. I think we are going back so soon because Father is too busy to be able to spend much time with us.

(Vienna) April 26th, 1880.

Father is going away again, to Paris this time. He says that it is a long journey, two nights and a day, but he doesn't mind that. Yesterday he said to Beckhoefer, who is now working for him at the *Neues Wiener Tagblatt*, that soon the trip to Paris will be much quicker, because they are going to build a new railway line across the Arlberg, that will bring France much nearer to Austria. I asked Father about this, and he said that it would be very important, " strategically and morally " he said, for France as well as us, and that's why the French are even prepared to help to pay for it.

15

He works hard for the Entente between us and France, and writes about it a great deal, and that is why he goes there so often. He knows all the important people in France, and often tells us about them—Charcot, who is a great scientist, Renan, a poet and philosopher, Jules Ferry, a politician, and Georges Clémenceau, another politician. But the man he likes best is Gambetta. He always speaks of him with admiration and affection. Only yesterday, when he was telling us about the railway and how he was going to Paris again, he said : " Gambetta is the great man of the French Republic. Now that republican France is established republicanism will spread throughout Europe."

Though I'm sorry that Father leaves us so often, I think he must have a very interesting time in France, and I wish we could go there with him. . . .

———————

Here I am inserting extracts from two of my father's meetings with Gambetta and Clémenceau. It was his habit always to write down a detailed account, often verbatim, as soon as possible after he had any important interview. I intend throughout the book to make use of these interviews, without any further introductory passages.

INTERVIEW WITH GAMBETTA, 15th May, 1880, 12.30— 1 p.m. Palais Bourbon

" Since I saw you last the result of the General Election in England has changed not only the Austrian situation, but the situation in the whole of Europe. Everywhere Liberal ideas have gained new strength. I understand that there are two lines of thought at the Court in Vienna, one mainly concerned with the re-establishment of the Holy Alliance. I believe that Austria may wish this, but I do not believe that Russia would like to renew the alliance of the three Emperors. As a matter of fact I am sure she will not do so. Further, I have been told that the Hungarians are very worried about the possible rapprochement between

16

Austria and Russia, and that their opposition to this might have quite a serious outcome. Well, as far as that is concerned, history has shown that, time and again, Austria has not taken Hungary's opinion into account; and if only Russia would be willing to enter into an alliance with Austria, that would be the case again; but as I have already said, such an alliance is out of the question. . . .

"You said that Count Taaffe was a very clever man, but 'a little reactionary'. A *little* reactionary for Austria perhaps, but for us '*un peu beaucoup*'." (I interjected: "That's where the difference between France and Austria lies.") "I have been told that the Slav idea is progressing in Austria, and you now say that the German Liberal parties are going to unite again, in order more efficiently to protect their principles. I am pleased to hear that. The German Liberals in Austria see that Germany is re-actionary, while the West is progressive. I have been flattered that I am, so to speak, the head of all the progressive parties of the Continent—*mais c'est un peu trop de besogne pour moi, j'en ai assez de diriger le parti liberal en France*."

*   *   *

"Boris Melikoff acts very cleverly in the internal pacification of Russia. It seems to me of great importance that, as you have told me, he has won over a section of the Russian emigrés in Geneva already. I think a reconciliation between Russia and Poland is possible. . . ."

*   *   *

"As I have often explained to you, I fully realize the import-ance of the Arlberg Tunnel. It is most likely that it will be built." (He meant that France would support the plan of a tunnel through the Arlberg, opening a new way for Austria towards the west both physically and financially.) "*Il est si facile de le faire, si on le veut seulement*."

*   *   *

"You said that the latest German developments are a proof that Bismarck has lost his position of absolute domination. I cannot share your opinion. The many little parties that make up the German Reichstag were all scared when Bismarck made his last move. As long as Bismarck remains the man of genius that he is, as long as some physical ailment doesn't make him irresponsible, he will rule Germany. (*Il gouvernera l'Allemagne en maître*.) The German parties are, to say the least of it, patient, and they will not revolt in the name of their Liberal principles against their lord (*maître*). Quite certainly they will not do so against Bismarck, though maybe they will later, against his successor. I have accurate information about Bismarck's physical condition. I had an opportunity of procuring a specimen of his handwriting lately. You know that one can draw conclusions about a man's condition from his handwriting. I have shown Bismarck's autograph to medical authorities. His writing" (and he made a gesture with his hand to show it) " does not run in straight lines, and is rather tremulous. That points, so the doctors assure me, to a neuropathic condition, perhaps brought about by the chronic alcoholism that has produced his sleeplessness. Insomnia can, as you quite rightly said, lead to a persecution mania. You must have noticed that for the last two years the Emperor Alexander has been a chronic alcoholic, without becoming insane, or going to the dogs. That is true, but Tsar Alexander *n'est pas le propriétaire de son cerveau. Il est seulement le locataire, il ne l'emploie pas comme le Chancellier de l'Allemagne.* He has no brains of his own, he uses other people's for his thinking, and consequently does not wear himself out like Bismarck. I cannot judge what will be the development of Bismarck's nervous condition. He is really a subject for clinical study, as you yourself pointed out in your paper, in the article called ' The Revenge of a Doctor ' on the 12th of May. As a matter of fact, Bismarck's last speech can only be discussed as a psychological study. It was a monologue, a kind of Hamlet-monologue (*un monologue à la Hamlet*). He spoke for himself only, and as soon as he finished he went away and left his party completely at a loss. It was a hopeless muddle (*gâchis*) and they could not find their way out (*ils n'ont pas pu trouver la boussole*).

" Nevertheless, whatever may be the likelihood of the Chancellor's future mental and physical state, at the moment Bismarck knows what he wants. You said that he is surrounded by internal difficulties and that there is a possibility that, like Napoleon III, he may try and make war outside Germany as a solution of those difficulties. Such a war could be directed against nobody but France. I don't believe in Bismarck's difficulties, and neither do I believe that he is in a position to declare war on France. At one time he wanted to, but he has missed the right moment. He may regret it now, but the time has passed. For this kind of undertaking the right moment and a favourable situation is needed (*il faut avoir pour des pareilles entreprises l'occasion et la bonne chance*). You said that the occasion might be re-created, but it is very hard to bring about the *bonne chance* too. That certainly is true, and that is why I believe that there can be no question of a German attack on France, although it is true that he bears France in mind in all his actions (*il vise toujours la France*).

" As far as we are concerned, we do not dream of a war with Germany and I would rather die (*je mourrais plutôt*) than permit an adventurous undertaking of that kind. One day the right time will come—*la France attendra son heure et son temps*."

Gambetta shook hands with me and asked me to call on him soon again.

INTERVIEW WITH CLÉMENCEAU, May 1st, 1880

(A copy of this was sent to the Crown Prince on October 8th, 1883.)

The Department of Justice, 6 p.m.

(Dr. Clémenceau practises medicine only amongst the poorest people. He is medium sized, supple, has short black hair with a few streaks of grey, moustache is still quite dark, olive complexion, black and lively eyes, talks quickly but distinctly, light baritone voice. Carelessly dressed, he had the obvious nervousness of a very busy man.)

19

Clémenceau told me :

" I understand that on the 23rd of May 2,500 workers will march from the Place de la Bastille to the Elysée and the Palais Bourbon, to invite Grévy and Gambetta to take the chair at the banquet given in honour of the Commune. It is quite a good idea, but I'm absolutely certain that it won't come to anything. The 23rd will pass off peacefully. This 23rd of May will pass peacefully, but God knows what will come in the future.

" Great changes will take place here in France. They must take place, for there is much, very much to be done before we attain a real Republic, a real democracy. The question is only, will these changes come about in a revolutionary way, or will they develop peacefully and legally. We are bogged in tradition. Take, for instance, the law of public meeting, and the press laws, which are at the moment being considered by the Commission. The Government does not want freedom of assembly, and it does not want freedom of the press—and the Government has the majority behind it. The present Government believes what previous Governments have believed—that it is not strong enough to permit freedom of meetings and the freedom of the press. To uphold the Government two great liberties must be withheld, liberties without which no real liberty is possible. But one day a Government must arise that will not be afraid of the freedom of the press, a Government that will permit anything to be written about it, which can stand every possible attack from the press, even the strongest, without wavering; and just because of this it will be strong, much stronger than all past Governments which have been frightened by journalists, and whose authority has been shattered by leading articles. On the day when we shall have that absolute freedom of the press in France, we shall have a really strong and authoritative Government, and at the same time we shall have the freedom which does not exist now. Monsieur Freycinet lacks the qualities of a political genius; he does not realize what can be done, what should be done, and what is essential to be done.

" I am still too young in politics and have not sufficient

political experience to give an opinion on foreign affairs. I certainly do not pretend to know Bismarck's plans and pretensions." (This appeared to be a hit against Gambetta.) " But I do know what France ought to do against Bismarck. Do you remember how the Prussians managed to take Paris? They didn't move until we had exhausted our provisions, and then we had to surrender. That is the way we ought to treat Bismarck. Remain quiet. Bismarck is surrounded by hundreds of difficulties, which will repeat themselves and increase, until from these difficulties real danger will develop. If Bismarck is not alive then, his successor will be, and I have the confident hope that we shall be able to take back that which is ours and which can never cease to be ours. That is my prediction of the course of the future. There is only one thing that worries me : France is called the land of the Commune. I for my part believe that Socialism is much more likely to come into power, and much sooner, in Russia and in Germany. Such an example could be momentous for France.

" I am informed about certain political combinations who want Bismarck to give us back Metz and Lorraine, while on the other hand the German provinces of Austria should be joined in a new German Bund. Bismarck's power would be increased by this. Metz and Lorraine would be worthless to us unless Alsace were included. But, even if they gave us both, we must consider carefully whether Austria should be dismembered in this way. It might be better to avoid this, and wait for the time when Alsace-Lorraine will be returned to us. Or even to make war to prevent the German provinces in Austria from being joined to Germany."

CHAPTER II

Paris, August 12th, 1880.

We have been a fortnight in France now. Father said that he would take us with him on condition that we stayed in the country near Paris. It is very nice here at the Pavillon Henri IV at St. Germain. . . . We have a manservant and Mother's own maid with us. So everything is very comfortable.

While we were going through the little garden at the back Father introduced Sofie and me to a gentleman who was sitting there, on a bench in the sun. In spite of the great heat he was all wrapped up in a big fur coat, as if he was freezing. He seemed very ill and fragile. His face was quite pale, and his eyebrows were white, so that they didn't show at all against the skin. It was odd to see such a colourless face surrounded by quite black hair. It looked like a shawl tied round his head instead of hair. In the midst of his white face was a black smear—his moustache. I couldn't make it out at first, then I suddenly realized that it was dyed, and so was his hair. He was Jacques Offenbach. I was ever so pleased because I had heard a lot about him, and knew his music.

He was most friendly to us. He smiled, held out his hands and took one of ours in each of his, and said : "I love Viennese girls. I'm sure you can both dance Viennese waltzes beautifully, well enough to make your partners quite dizzy. Vienna! . . ." He sighed. "What a charming place, what a wonderful place to live in. . . . Vienna and its music are inseparable. You cannot think of Vienna without thinking of my friend Johann Strauss's immortal waltzes; the tune of the ' Blue Danube ' will last as long as the river. . . . If you see Johann Strauss greet him very heartily from his admirer Offenbach."

22

Adèle, Vienna

MORITZ SZEPS

I think it is very nice that Offenbach, who is such a great composer himself, should so willingly acknowledge the greatness of Johann Strauss. Perhaps really great men never envy each other's fame.

We are going to have the house full of great men next autumn. There will be a big international writers' congress in Vienna, and my father has been discussing it with a lot of French authors here. He told me that after the congress there will be a reception at our house, with more than four hundred guests, and the new stage that is being built for our private theatricals will be ready in time for the reception.

(Vienna) October 11th, 1880.

To-morrow the big reception at our house will take place. We are very excited. People from all over Europe will be coming. The stage has been finished and is in the biggest of the reception rooms. I am going to be a kind of stage manager, and will have to draw the curtain and help as much as possible behind the scenes. Sofie is too grand and grown up nowadays to do anything like that. She is going to help Mother; I think she fancies herself playing the hostess.

My father has chosen the programme himself. He decided on the comedy *Toto chez Tata* because it is in both French and German. The Frenchwoman's part is going to be played by Stella Hohenfels. I think she is by far the best of the Burgtheater actresses. Friedrich Mitterwurzer will be the leading man. I cannot say how thrilled I am at the thought of meeting him. They say he is the greatest actor since Garrick; they also say that he is a little mad. I have never met him before, but I have heard so much about him that I feel I know all about him already.

But even more of a sensation than the play will be the surprise that Father has prepared. He has had some strange-looking machinery fixed up in the house, and all the rooms and the garden are going to be lit by electricity. I have never seen the electric light before, and I don't think there are any houses in Vienna which have it. . . .

(Vienna) October 13th.

It is all over. And what a success! It was the most interesting party for years, everyone agreed about that. My uncle said it was a collection of "lords of the spirit". I cannot start to put down a list of the names of the famous people who came, because it would include the whole four hundred guests. I think it's perfectly correct to say that everyone had a wonderful time—with the exception of two people : Mitterwurzer and me.

My troubles were due to the play. To Mitterwurzer and his temperament in fact. He was very nice and friendly when I met him, and quite ordinary. He and the Hohenfels were standing in the middle of the stage waiting for the curtain to be drawn. And I was waiting for the signal to draw the curtain. Only this curtain had a little hole in it, so that the actors could peep through at the audience before the scenes began. Well, Mitterwurzer went up to it and took a long look. Suddenly he turned round, tore off his wig, and said that he would not go on. " I won't go on with that creature in front. I've had enough of him. It's bad enough having to put up with him at the theatre, he's got no business here. . . ." And so on, and so forth. He had seen, sitting in the front row of the audience, the director, Freiherr von Dingelstedt. And, as everyone knows, they were hardly on speaking terms, and always quarrelled violently when they did speak.

So the Hohenfels begins to cry, while Mitterwurzer stands in the middle of the stage brandishing his wig. Crisis. The audience, unsuspecting, sits and waits for the curtain to go up. And I am holding on to the curtain rope feeling most unhappy and wondering what to do.

I don't know what gave me the courage to begin drawing the curtain. I felt that Mitterwurzer was too much of an actor to walk off the stage once he faced the audience.

I was right. As he heard the curtain beginning to open he jammed on his wig and began to bow to the frantically clapping audience. But during the applause I distinctly heard a loud whisper coming from him, and I am quite certain that the director, to whom his remark was addressed, must have heard it too : " I'll build a prompter's box from your bones one of these days, you assassin. . . ."

I did not stop shaking for some time, and was glad that Mother permitted me to drink one glass of champagne. . . .

(Vienna) October 28th, 1880.

. . . to-day, while we were sitting in Father's library after lunch, the butler announced Professor Carl Menger. He has often been to the house before, and has spoken to my father about Crown Prince Rudolf, whose tutor and friend he is. (He is also a famous economist, my father says.) He said the Crown Prince had sent him, to ask him to arrange an interview between him (the Crown Prince) and my father. To-day Menger said that Rudolf wanted to have direct contact with the leading men of the country. And he said that not only was my father one of these leading men, " but through his leaders in the *Neues Wiener Tagblatt*, the leader of many of the other ' leading men ' in Austria ". I was proud to hear him say this to my father.

They arranged for my father to meet Crown Prince Rudolf to-night. Rudolf usually lives in Prague, and though he quite often comes to Vienna he only stays here for a short time.

For the next eight years, until the tragedy of the Crown Prince's end, Moritz Szeps and Rudolf used either to write or to see each other at least once a week. My father, who was much older (the Crown Prince died at the age of thirty-two), exercised a profound influence on his intellectual and political development. Rudolf who, like his idealistic mother, the Empress Elizabeth, had from his early childhood revolted against the narrow-minded clerical and reactionary atmosphere of the Imperial court, found at last a congenial friend and instructor in my father. Through him he was able to understand the real spirit of democracy; proof of this was demonstrated by his growing interest in the Western democracies, especially in the young French Republic.

My father followed a constant Francophile policy in his paper which was strengthened through his friendship with Gambetta, and, later, through the family bonds that united him with Georges Clémenceau. And this policy found an ardent adherent in Rudolf.

The Crown Prince was in his early twenties, but his education and knowledge were greatly superior to those of most of his royal contemporaries, who were destined to make world history at the end of the nineteenth century. At the same time he was a noble and lovable character, who won all hearts. His first official tour abroad, undertaken in 1878, after his coming of age, was to England. There he charmed the unbending Queen Victoria, who, as a sign of her favour, even asked him to Osborne. " He'll be a success " was the prophecy of Lord Beaconsfield, and the joke went round the court that the Queen had fallen in love with the young Rudolf.

His sister-in-law, the Princess of Coburg, sister of Crown Princess Stephanie, sketched a portrait of his character : " He was more than beautiful. He was enchanting. Behind his fragile appearance lay reserves of strength and energy. He reminded one of a race-horse; he had its temperament, breeding and caprice. His will-power was only equalled by his sensibility. His pale face mirrored all his feelings. His shining brown eyes seemed to change their very colour and shape as often as the expression of his face altered. A caressing look would change into a glare of hatred, yet in an instant be transformed into a caress again. . . . Like his mother, the Empress Elizabeth, he had a way of talking that held everybody, and a faculty of setting all about him agog to solve the riddle of his personality."

The impressions of early childhood are often decisive for a man. On the 5th of July, 1866, the Crown Prince learned, in a letter from his mother, of the fatal defeat of Köeniggraetz. The eight-year-old boy was deeply conscious of the disgrace inflicted upon Austria by the Hohenzollerns. In a poem which Count

Latour found later among his lesson books, the boy gave vent to his intense desire for revenge. " God's fist will crush the Hohenzollerns for Köeniggraetz and Sedan," runs the concluding line. An antipathy for Prussia coloured his political thinking until his death.

Another insight into the development of the boy is given, seven years later, by a scrappy diary.

" I realize that I can never know everything that I desire to know. But one thing is sure, that one must fight and strive for more and more knowledge, not for titles, nor honours, nor money. No! leave these to the mercenary families. . . . I want to *know* ! "

He continues :

" The kingdom exists only in the sense that a mighty ruin lingers on from day to day, but in the end must fall. It existed for centuries, and as long as the people suffered themselves to be led blindly, it stood firm. But its task is at an end now. All men are free, and the ruin must collapse with the next storm."

Before he started out on his second tour abroad, in 1879, this time to Spain, the young man, as if the idea of death were constantly in his mind, wrote out a testament. It reads like the spiritual bequest of a wise and mature man, and yet it is only the confession of one scarcely adult. " I forgive my enemies. I forgive all those who have worried me, especially of late; I have been following a different path from that of my forbears, but I too have nothing but the purest motives. Our time demands new ideas. Everywhere reaction is the prelude to downfall, but especially is it so in Austria. Those who preach reaction are the most dangerous foes. I have always opposed them. Beware of them ! "

His mother, the Empress Elizabeth, had a profound affection for King Ludwig the Second of Bavaria. And her feelings were shared by her son, who was deeply attached to this solitary and melancholy man. They were united in their hatred of Prussia, and they both prophetically named her " the scourge of Europe ". Rudolf was fascinated by King Ludwig, and the King of Bavaria was so fond of the Crown Prince that the festivities which he arranged in his honour became almost legendary. The much-talked-about reception at the Winter Garden, in 1880, where fabulous wealth was displayed, was held expressly in honour of Rudolf. Yet in the midst of it all the two royalties spent the night secluded—deep in philosophical discourse. Only years later did it become apparent that the first seeds of Rudolf's profound disregard for life were planted in his youthful soul by King Ludwig during their conversations. When Ludwig's melancholy later developed into insanity the Crown Prince was deeply perturbed by this. But for the Empress Elizabeth the fate of her nephew, the King of Bavaria, meant a renewal of the nightmares that had been torturing her for many years. She wrote to a friend : " Perhaps I, even now, have transmitted to my descendants the disastrous taint of the Wittelsbachers; this tenor never leaves me."

These brief notes on the Crown Prince are intended to serve as a background for a description of the friendship between him and my father. Their friendship was not the result of pure chance. They had a common thirst for knowledge. Both had an almost instinctive dislike and distrust of the Prussians. And mutual hatred of all reactionary ideas, accompanied by a fully conscious democratic ideal, drew them together.

CHAPTER III

DIARY

(*Vienna*) *August 15, 1881.*

. . . my father has been having a lot of correspondence with Gambetta lately. There is going to be a general election in France. Father says that it will be of European importance. A Liberal victory will mean a victory for the cause of Liberalism everywhere. It is of special importance for Gambetta of course, and Father is going to France to-morrow to discuss it with him. . . .

INTERVIEW WITH GAMBETTA, August 21st, 1881, 2 p.m.
Palais Bourbon

Outwardly Gambetta was quite quiet about the chances of the election, as if he was either certain of its outcome or didn't care about it. But, right at the end of our interview, he said: " You know, even if I don't get a majority, nothing much will be changed." (*Il n'y a rien de change.*)

I interjected that this was an important day for Europe, that it was not only a Parisian, a French, but a European election. Gambetta agreed that the election could be regarded as an important factor in the history of Liberalism. " Germany will have a General Election too. What do you think about it? What will be the result? By the way, I'd like to tell you an odd story. I had a long talk with Lasker a few days ago, in Heligoland. He developed the idea that in no circumstances whatever can the German Liberals let Bismarck fall. Bismarck was the man destined by history to prevent the dominance of the Gallic race, of the Gallic species."

" What, Lasker! Is that how he speaks of the originator of anti-semitism? "

" That's so. And although all the varying shades of Liberal opinion in Germany have decided on common action, they don't want to bring down Bismarck. Sonnemann was the only one who frankly declared in his paper that if they were to act on Parliamentary principles, the opposition would have openly to ask for Bismarck's resignation. But leaving that aside, what does Lasker mean by the Gallic race? Has anyone ever seen the difference between the blood corpuscles of the Gallic race and those of the German race? What is a race, anyhow, and what does Lasker mean by it?

" Well-informed circles contend that the Liberals will keep their Parliamentary seats, but Bismarck is prepared for such a contingency. With the Ultramontanes he will have the majority anyway, or perhaps it would be better to say that the majority will have him. Bismarck's whole system is: the care of the nation should be the noble families and the Junkers (*les hoberaus*). That's what it amounts to. The army and the civil service should rest entirely in their hands. And he wants to have his Junkers everywhere, in Hamburg too. The masses allow themselves to be spat on by them, without revolting. They are too stupid (*trop bêtes*).

" If ever we had a war with Germany and we were victorious, we would not commit the folly of asking for a war indemnity of many milliards, and create an economic breakdown such as Germany created in France. The war indemnity would have to be paid by the Junkers. Their estates and their latifundia would be parcelled out and allotted to the German people, and we would declare this quite openly at the beginning of the war. . . .

" Bismarck will certainly use every pretext for conscripting more soldiers, producing more cannon and rifles, and asking for more and more money. I wonder who will first give out in this race. In the next war the bullets fired will be golden ones. It was a great Austrian, your General Montecuccoli, who said that for a successful war there are three things necessary—' the first is money, the second is more money, and the third and last is nothing else but money.' "

To that I replied: "No one but an Austrian could have said that. We Austrians know the value of money for the simple reason that we have never yet had enough of it."

Gambetta laughed, and asked me to come with him that evening to the meeting of the Central Committee at 25 rue de Suresnes.

Our interview ended at 2.30 p.m., and I went straight to the Restaurant de la Cascade, Bois de Boulogne, to write down these notes.

INTERVIEW WITH GAMBETTA, November 2nd, 1881, 4.40 to 6 p.m.

Gambetta began to talk about King Humbert of Italy's conversations with the Emperor Francis Joseph. "Humbert is an enemy of France. He is by no means a *friend* of Germany, but, I repeat, first and foremost he is an enemy of France. That makes an enormous difference. Humbert now feels certain that, since I have come to power, a war between well-armed Germany and democratic, peace-loving France cannot be avoided. I know, from very well-informed sources, that he expects such a war to take place quite shortly. He believes that France will be crushed (*écrasé*) and he hurries to the side of the likely victors to make sure of a share of the loot. What miserable creatures they are! They don't realize that once I'm in power nothing will be allowed to involve us in war. No one wants peace as much as I do. Bismarck wants the Italians for vassals—for what else can Italy be to Germany. As well as that, the Italians have to promise to be ' good children ' and finish with all their revolutionary ideas and their ' *Terra irredenta* '. They have to shift their political aspirations from the East to the West. I am sure the day will come when the House of Savoy is going to realize what a mistake they have made in their calculations; the day will come when they will have a bone to pick with their ally (Germany) and they won't find them as friendly as were their enemies."

Then Gambetta began to talk about his travels through Germany. . . . He said he was really impressed by the discipline that prevailed there. His main strategical impressions were:

1. The whole of the Baltic and North Sea coasts were well fortified and could be defended against even the strongest attacks.

2. The Eastern frontiers are much more highly developed than the Western. The strength of the defence against Russia is much greater than that against the West. And anyhow, he said, an alliance between Germany and Russia would have no value whatever. Russia can only be a field of conquest for Germany, while she herself will never try to conquer Germany.

Germany no longer needs the Netherlands, and most likely no longer has any aspirations concerning them.

He then went on about the pleasure he had in finding himself unrecognized throughout his stay in Germany. Only at Dagny-sur-Moselle, on his way back, the station-master recognized him and shouted enthusiastically " *Vive la République! Vive Gambetta!* " He said that he would have to find himself a new name the next time he went travelling incognito. The name Massabie was already rather worn out.

We then went on to speak of the choice of Ministers he had made for his Cabinet. He said: " I have chosen young men, men who can work, and men who are unanimously agreed about the execution of the necessary reforms." He pointed out that all the row that had been kicked up about the possible changes in the French railway system was simply ridiculous. " It's true that I want improvements and modifications. A lowering of tariffs, and the strictest execution of the clauses of the *cashier de charge*. I cannot bother about a few rich shareholders as long as the public approves of my actions. The old slipshod ways here and everywhere else must stop. I'm going to make an end to the situation of a state within the state, set up by a few wealthy oligarchs. These gentlemen must get used to recognizing the sovereignty of the state, and must cease opposing it at every step."

All this gave me the impression that Gambetta has abandoned the idea of nationalizing the French railways. He ended by saying: " You won't publish what I told you about the railways, will you? " And he put his fingers to his lips. " *C'est entendu.*"

CHAPTER IV

DIARY

. . . Ever since my father has been in touch with the Crown
Prince I have been his secretary. The Crown Prince's letters are
strictly confidential and secret, dangerous both for the writer and
the recipient. My training as Father's helper is now proving
useful. I alone am empowered to receive the letters, and to
forward their answers. It is interesting and responsible work;
the one thing about it that I don't like is that I have to get up
so early. Father has his breakfast now at half-past seven, because
old Nehammer usually arrives at the house by eight. This old
servant is the only person who has the Prince's unlimited confidence. He adores his master and the poor frail old chap tries
to guard him whenever possible.

The Erzherzog's intrigues against Rudolf are really disgusting! Nehammer has to be frightfully careful, make detours,
change his tram two or three times, all because he has to shake
off the detective who always tries to follow him. Of course our
servants cannot be allowed to know who Nehammer is, so Father
has told the porter that the doctor has ordered me to be massaged,
so that Nehammer can come to my room without rousing any
suspicions.

" From his Imperial Highness " were the words with which
he handed me a letter yesterday. Father and I read it together.
It really is a shame that the Emperor allows himself to be so
influenced against his son, and that he should let him be excluded
from every political move.

Father thinks that Rudolf has the brains and power to see
the connections between the various European political under-
currents, and that he is predestined to become a great statesman.
It makes me sad to see this man write : " At home I am so

excluded from political information that I have no control whatever over the correctness of my own impressions." . . .

. . . His letters come in a big square envelope, sealed with
three seals. And Father answers them straight away. . . .

———————

Moritz Szeps became more and more intimate with the Crown
Prince. Through his influence Rudolf became a European
statesman. My father's letters were the vehicle of regular instructions in the contemporary events of European politics and their
significance; and very soon the gifted Crown Prince was enabled
to develop a definite political point of view.

Examples of his development can be seen in his letters.

Prague, June 2nd, 1882.

Dear Mr. Szeps,

It might be of interest to you to publish in your paper an
item of news, before the other papers receive it. In regard to the
baptism of the young Prussian Prince. Our Emperor and I will
be the godfathers. I am to arrive there on the morning of the
11th, to represent our Emperor as well as myself, at the " god-
fatherly " festivity. It is most likely that my wife will accompany
me to Berlin. We shall arrive on the 11th in the morning and
play our role at the baptism at Potsdam, which will take place
on the same day. We shall have to stay until the evening of
the 12th. We should like to be back by the morning of the
13th, but we are not sure yet.

You may use all this, but please do it in a way that does not
compromise me—perhaps as a message from Berlin. If it were
known that this note came from me, it would entail a lot of
disagreeable discussions.

One christening is like another; a festive one more boring
than a quiet one. But this particular affair, on the 11th June in
Berlin, has a very serious background. These unheard-of embraces between the Viennese and the Berlin courts are brought
about by the alliance of the Western powers, by the happy,

wealthy, powerful French republic, which proved itself able to survive and now stands, scarcely twelve years after Sedan, as an undeniably obvious proof that European republics can perform great tasks. And Russia, lying in the convulsions of delirium tremens, is lost as a support for the Conservative principles of the Holy Alliance. It is that which brings the Conservative courts of Vienna and Berlin together; it is that which compels their embraces; that, as I have said, gives the baptismal font a very serious and interesting background.

Many greetings,

Yours,

RUDOLF.

Prague, July 26th, 1882.

DEAR MR. SZEPS,

I am returning you the two books which you were kind enough to lend me, with my warmest thanks. Both were very interesting to me. The one about Nihilism is the very best that I have yet seen dealing with the situation in Russia, which is so difficult for us Europeans to understand. The second one, perhaps, is even more attractive. It is likely that the difference between Italy and France will become more obvious from day to day through these Egyptian complications. The example is very instructive : with really highly developed peoples the principles of nationalism and racial cohesion recede into the background in favour of questions of politics and power. The principle of nationalism is erected upon the basest and most bestial foundations; it really means victory of the carnal instincts and feelings over spiritual civilization. The latter brings equality to all peoples, cosmopolitism for the human race. I regard national and racial hatred as a big step backwards; and it is significant enough that just those elements in Europe which are most against progress, are most devoted to these principles, and exploit them for their own ends. As science is cosmopolitan, all parts of human society will in time have to become inter-related.

Without wanting to offend Count Taaffe we in Austria are not yet quite set on the path that will lead us to this golden age.

I am extremely interested in this Egyptian entanglement as I know the country very well and expected the situation to develop in this way years ago.

What these complications on the Nile will lead to in European politics is unforeseeable. If Arabi[1] were *the* Moslem since Suliman—which, in spite of his much-talked-about energy, he is not—the English and French could be disastrously defeated in a shameful campaign.

For many long evenings last winter whilst we were on the Nile steamer I spoke to an intimate friend of mine, Abd el Kader Pasha, who is a mixture of the Ottoman and Arabic races and unites in himself the extreme fanaticism of both peoples, about the things that were really happening now, and what could be done about a European invasion.

Arabi could have at his disposal an enormous fighting power, but apparently he doesn't know how to use it.

Count K.[2] is a great diplomat! His remark that the bombardment of Alexandria[3] was a real decision in the eyes of the English, but that the continuation of this action, which might have saved the unfortunate town from disaster, would not have been a fair undertaking, was immense.

What a pity Europe wastes so much money on her diplomats. God knows the harm they do is much greater than the good.

Prague, November 19th, 1882.

DEAR MR. SZEPS,

. . . I shall be very pleased to learn something from you about France, as a peculiar situation must have arisen there. I have for that country . . . great sympathies. We are indebted to France

[1] Arabi Pasha was the leader of the Egyptian revolution in 1882 which led to the English intervention. On September 13th, 1882, he was beaten at Tel-el-Kebir by Wolseley and captured by the English.
[2] Count K. is Count Kalnoky, the Austro-Hungarian Minister of Foreign Affairs from November 1881 to May 1895.
[3] The bombardment of Alexandria was the first step in the English intervention in Egypt. A great part of the town was destroyed, and numerous people, mostly Europeans, were killed by the shelling and some by the looting mob.

as the source of all the Liberal ideas and constitutions in Europe. And whenever great ideas begin to ferment, France will be looked to for an example. What is Germany compared with her? Nothing but an enormously enlarged Prussian regimental barbarism, a purely military state. . . .

What advantage did Germany get from 1870? . . . to all . . . their little kings and princes has been added an Emperor. They have to pay for a bigger army. And the idea of the Reich's unity supported by police and civil servants, of a drilled patriotism, learned by heart, is held up in the air above the points of fixed bayonets. What would contemporary Germany be like after a military defeat by republican France? What would it do if the army began to waver? The good Germans would begin to sing " *Allons enfants de la Patrie* ", as they did at the end of the last century. Although France now seems asleep, she holds a leading position; and that is what will make the socialist movement, already developing into Anarchism, a serious problem once it develops into a great force there. The rest of Europe has enough of these elements waiting for a signal. Look what progress the Socialist Party has made here in the course of a few years. In Bohemia its members and sympathizers are the only people who disregard all national differences for the sake of higher aims. Germans and Czechs work together there.

If you would let me know your opinion of the Socialist movements in France and at home, and especially about the Viennese excesses at the Neubau, I should be very grateful to you indeed.

A heavy and murky atmosphere hangs over Europe. It is not a really vehement illness, but everybody feels " louse ". There is a fear both of an internal eruption, and of one from without.

I am allowed to speak because I belong to those who are officially the least well-informed people in Austria. So what I say is my private opinion : I believe that the ghosts of war are walking again, and that the definite annexation of Bosnia and Herzegovina is desired.

A Russian war is the great nightmare.

38

Germany, too, is very concerned about this. Although the following is only a little incident, one can see from it that they want to remain on the most intimate terms with us. As you know, since July I have been twice to Prussia. Now I have another invitation from the old Emperor to come to Berlin on the 30th November, and to go out shooting with him at Letzlingenzu. I have been ordered from Budapest to accept it, and so I must make yet a third pilgrimage in such a short time. Prussia is friendly only when she needs somebody.

I believe that very serious times are approaching. . . .

Although at this time there was an official alliance between Germany and Austria, Bismarck was very well aware that once Rudolf came to the throne Austria would take its stand beside the Western democracies.

Because of the fundamentally different Prussian ideology the ordinary Austrian, and even the Emperor, did not feel happy that their country should be tied to Germany. It was felt that Austria could only be happy and strong as a free federation of its many constituent races. So Bismarck had his doubts about the durability of the 1878 agreement, and wanted it to be ratified by the parliaments in Berlin, Vienna and Budapest. A storm of protest against this proposal arose throughout Austria. Perhaps the clearest insight into this situation can be given from my father's account of an interview with the Crown Prince.

INTERVIEW WITH THE CROWN PRINCE (December 29th, 1882, at the Hofburg, Vienna)

The Crown Prince received me at three in the afternoon. He was more nervous and upset than I had ever seen him before. He began with a lament over the failure of the Hapsburg day.[1] And he went on discussing this theme uninterruptedly for nearly an hour. At such a time as the present, every opportunity to

[1] The Hapsburg day was the yearly reunion of all the members of the Hapsburg family from all parts of the world.

strengthen the people's feelings for the dynasty should be seized. Well-arranged and imposing ceremonies would not only have helped this, but they would also have been useful from the point of view of our relations with Berlin. " But all logic is useless—everything is relegated to the background for fear that Count Taaffe may lose his Bohemian followers." He doesn't dare to make any move, and that is the reason why the Hapsburg day was dull and colourless. It really was a scandal. It would have been so easy to have made it different. If only the order had been given for the whole court to go on a ceremonial procession, similar to that of the Corpus Christi procession, all Vienna would have been looking on. The Viennese have watched this procession six hundred times, and it still draws the same crowds. What on earth is the use of all those picturesque clothes, the state coaches, the Spanish white horses and the Guards, if they are not shown off on such an occasion, when they could have a big moral effect. It would be better not to have them at all. And if only the Emperor had ordered a gala in the big Redouten-Saal, instead of the rather shabby court dinner that actually took place, there would have been plenty of deputations and the highest aristocracy could not have stayed apart. As you realize, the whole of the old nobility—which really leads Austria now—were pointedly absent both from the church ceremony and at court on the day. They wanted to show that they really didn't need the court any more. But apart from those aristocrats, the fear of the middle class that Vienna would become a provincial town was apparent. If one only knew what could be done for Vienna!

Pest is in the midst of growing, there is real life there, and if it continues in the same way for another two decades it will far surpass Vienna. And, compared with Vienna, even Prague is beginning to be a real centre.

Then the Crown Prince returned again to the theme of the Hapsburg day, and asked me if I could publish some of his views on it. I said that I would try and do so in the New Year's Eve issue, but I was afraid that if the article were properly written it would be confiscated by the police. And if it were not written in this way it would be weak and colourless.

Then followed a new and important subject. " I had Count Kalnoky brought to me to-day, and I will tell you right away what my reasons were. He was with me for a long time and, just imagine it : at the very beginning of our talk he declared that to-day, the 29th of December, 1882, he had acquired the conviction that Bismarck himself was really behind the whole newspaper campaign about the Austro-German Alliance. So it is only to-day that our Minister of Foreign Affairs has realized what every cab-driver who reads his paper with the slightest intelligence must have known for the last fortnight. And, as if to excuse himself, Count Kalnoky added that Prince Reuss too had only to-day come to the same conclusion, and the whole time he (Kalnoky) was talking to Prince Reuss, he was nodding his head incredulously, affirming that he had no instructions and no news from Berlin, and he really did not know what was going on. Well, those two are really suitable companions.

" But the reason I had sent for Count Kalnoky was not to hear this. I said to him : ' My dear Count, I understand from a well-informed source that you have again got some plan for me : someone put me wise to it that you want to send me to Berlin again. And so I would like to hear this from yourself.' Kalnoky answered that although it was not yet decided, it would, as a matter of fact, be highly desirable if my Royal Highness would go to Berlin to fulfil an important political mission. So I pointed out to Kalnoky—' Let us look at the purely formal side of it for a moment. I cannot very well go to Berlin without being invited.'

" ' An excuse could be found,' answered Kalnoky. As a matter of fact one has been found already. In Berlin the celebration of the Crown Prince's silver wedding will shortly take place. And as my Royal Highness was on very good terms with them, especially with their elder son, an invitation could be easily arranged.

" So I took out the letter I had received from Prince Wilhelm

a few days ago, and said to Count Kalnoky : ' Now look at
what my friend has written to me : it'll be only an intimate
family affair, the main feature will be living statues posed for
by the Hohenzollerns. Here is a list of the actors. And now,
my dear Count Kalnoky, tell me, do you know what living
statues really are? '

" The Count answered : ' Oh, yes, historical tableaux.'

" ' Quite right,' I said. ' You certainly must remember the
ones that we posed for at the silver wedding of the Austrian
majesties. They were all concerned with the past glories of
our imperial house and of Austria. Now, dear Count Kalnoky,
if you take world history into account, what kind of living
statues could they pose for in Berlin? You certainly won't
assume that on such an occasion they will revive the memory
of Jena and Auerstäedt. The Prussians have only two glorious
days in which we have no part. They are—Sedan and Versailles.
But they only make two pictures, and that's not enough. To
complete the necessary half-dozen they must have four more.
They have no other choice left but the first Silesian war, the
conquest of Silesia, the Seven Years War, and many others of
this sort. But always we have a part in them. For the whole
history of Prussia up to Sedan has been nothing but the robbery
of Austrian soil for the benefit of Prussia, either by a process
of slow undermining, or by sudden seizures. These, my dear
Count Kalnoky, will be the subject of the living statues.

" ' Now I must ask you, what is your opinion of my assisting
at such a performance. Personally I really wouldn't mind it,
because I accept the facts of history; I believe bygones to be
bygones. But those who offer me hospitality, and who would
like to show me some kindness, might be upset by it. And
you will certainly understand that that must be the reason why
Prince Wilhelm's friendly letter about the silver wedding does
not end with an invitation to be present there.' "

The Crown Prince added, " This historical lecture may be
of use to Count Kalnoky." And then he continued, " What
really lies behind all this is Bismarck's idea of strengthening

and making lasting the Austro-German Alliance, by giving it the legal blessing of the parliaments of Vienna, Berlin and Pest. That was already in Bismarck's mind in 1878. And when he came to Vienna in '79 he was quite open about it. But at that time the Emperor didn't want to discuss it, and Bismarck vigorously complained about this, as well as about the fact that there was a strong feeling in Vienna against the alliance. He appears to have abandoned the idea for some time afterwards. It seems that he now has some reason for returning to it. And it further seems that they have chosen me to act as an intermediary. I will read you a most peculiar letter that I received yesterday, and which really made me send for Kalnoky to-day."

The Crown Prince took from his portfolio some bluish octavo sheets, five pages of which were covered with a virile handwriting and, incidentally, with many alterations and corrections in the same hand. The letter began with the words " Dear Rudolf ". (As far as I am able I reproduce the letter verbatim, and those parts which I cannot remember exactly I have made a précis of.) The following are the contents of this unusual letter, which in many ways bears the character of a state paper, and which come from the Emperor's aged uncle, Erzherzog Albrecht :

" DEAR RUDOLF,

" I understand that they intend to send you to Berlin again, so that you can discuss the ideas originated by Fürst Bismarck, i.e. that the Austro-German Alliance should be raised by the parliaments of Austria, Germany and Hungary to the status of a law. In this important situation I am addressing the following lines to you. You will be confronted in Berlin with a genius, and an extremely subtle and experienced man. In order that you in your youthfulness may be cautious in judging his character and his intentions, I should like to remind you of an incident of which you yourself have spoken. Bismarck once told you confidentially that, in 1876, when King

43

Wilhelm wanted to take Bohemia from us, it was he (Bismarck) who held him back. Bismarck obviously wanted to win you over by this, and to show his moderation and friendship. But to make quite sure of you, Fürst Bismarck did not refrain from, so to speak, throwing suspicion upon his royal master. The memory of this should be a warning to you."

The letter then continues with a discussion of the following problems : " The power of the Crown is becoming very limited, but the right to declare war and conclude peace undeniably still rests with it, as indeed it does with the highest authority of the State even in republics. Parliaments have nothing else to do (in the case of war) except to vote for the necessary financial measures, and to accept the fact. If the Austro-German Alliance is ratified by the three parliaments, then they will be in a position where they can undeniably and definitely challenge the rights of Sovereigns to declare war and conclude peace. Thus royal powers will be still further limited. But there are also other possible consequences of this; it might happen that these three parliaments in the future could not agree about political questions arising from this alliance. Situations similar to those that arose in the old German Bundesversammlung, where Austria and Russia took part, would necessarily arise again. These differences in the Bundesversammlung were one of the main causes of the tension between Austria and Prussia, finally leading to the decisive war, which, it is true, Austria began at the worst possible moment for herself. It is therefore reasonable to fear that the Austro-German Alliance might not only be weakened, but in the end might lead to a new armed conflict between the two powers, through the apparent strengthening that it would now receive by the parliamentary ratifications. Austria is weakened as a result of the occupation of Bosnia, and such a conflict would necessarily find it in an unfavourable position. We cannot take the path leading to Constantinople, which is the logical consequence of the occupation of Bosnia, because it would mean a further weakening. We have not enough strength to incorporate the savage and uncivilized Balkan nations in our state in a form that would lead to a real increase in our power.

" One should further consider," continues the letter, " that while there is a united parliament in Germany, there are two parliaments in Austro-Hungary, often pursuing different ends; so that from such an alliance it would really follow that the German parliament and the German government would be the dominating factors. The Austrians would, in effect, become second-class Prussians. The Hapsburg domains would soon come under the Sovereignty of Germany. The time for the fulfilment of Hungary's wish for a direct personal union would have come. Think over carefully what would then happen to our old Monarch. There is nothing that Austria has to fear more than ' *Deutschnationales Cabinet* '. But even if this would not eventuate, the realization of Bismarck's ideas would have the same consequences for us.

" You are the Crown Prince, so it is especially important for you to consider these things. Be careful, therefore. It really would be best if you could keep aloof from the whole affair, and not go as an intermediary to Berlin. At the present moment political reasons may be so compelling that we shall be forced to accept Bismarck's ideas. But you should have nothing to do with it. Otherwise if it happened you would have been personally involved in it, and would have to remain personally involved in it. I feel it my duty, as the oldest member of the family, to tell you all this before you make a decision. Behave so as not to endanger your own future and the future of our house.

" Your faithful uncle,
" ALBRECHT."

A postscript was added in which he explained the history of the last hundred years of Poland's existence, to show that the interference of foreign states with the internal politics of a country is inevitably followed by its downfall. Such interference with Austria would undoubtedly be attempted if the German Parliament and the German Government secured, through the above-mentioned alliance, the right to interfere.

The Crown Prince said to me : " And now I beg you to tell me your opinion, and advise me what to do."

I answered him on the following lines : Although I usually did not agree with Erzherzog Albrecht's point of view, I had to admit that most of what he had written was only too true. (The Crown Prince nodded agreement.) One thing is certain—if you make your appearance on the scene in Berlin, you are personally responsible for it now and in the future. But this is not my only fear. You must, if you mediate at all, be certain of success. The problem is the Austrian and Hungarian parliamentary ratification. The Hungarian parliament will accept it; but before you went to Berlin you would have to get an absolute guarantee from Count Taaffe that the Austrian parliament will accept it too. The situation here is not as safe as in Pest—Poles, Czechs, Slovenes, and perhaps the southern nations, might all vote against it. As you know, only a part of the present majority would be needed to form, with the present compact minority, a new block for the Alliance. It is by no means certain that the entire left wing will vote for the Alliance. Within the German party in Austria there may be more than one deputy who would be against a complete absorption by Germany. Apart from that, it could happen that those left wingers who favour this alliance might vote against it as long as it is sponsored by Count Taaffe, with the aim merely of making the present government fall. They might make a reservation that they would vote for it if it were sponsored by another Cabinet. Now it is obviously a difficult thing for your Royal Highness to work for a project and to expose yourself personally to the danger that it might not be accepted by your own parliament. Even if we disregard the fact that such a failure would be to the personal detriment of Your Highness, we must not forget that such a rejection by parliament would lead to a tension between the two countries, a tension that might bring about a fatal war, for which Your Highness would share the responsibility. Therefore, I must repeat that it is of the

utmost importance to have an absolute guarantee by Count
Taaffe that a majority of the Austrian parliament will vote
favourably. And I am by no means sure that a two-thirds
majority would not be necessary for such a law, as it might be
regarded as an alteration of the constitution.

After a short pause for reflection the Crown Prince answered :
" You are right, that will be the best thing. Count Taaffe must
furnish this guarantee."

I answered : " Count Taaffe would doubtless give all possible
promises, but that wouldn't be enough."

The Crown Prince replied : " Certainly not. I know Count
Taaffe to be a rather easy-going gentleman, and I'll certainly
insist on positive guarantees. I do wonder, however, whether
and how he will succeed in furnishing any." And the Crown
Prince smiled, very pleased with himself. Some other remarks
that he made in the course of the conversation are :

" Count Tisza seems to be very much displeased with Count
Kalnoky. The assurances of the Foreign Minister, which he had
communicated to Pest, were not fully credited there. They were
that he (Kalnoky) clings absolutely to the German alliance, and
does not dream about the rapprochement with Russia.

" Tisza's remarks to me about the Taaffe Government and the
present system were proof of his annoyance. He said that the
moment will come when the Hungarians will have to stand up
against the Taaffe Government. The Hungarians were especially
worried and angry about the Czechs, who had tried to ' Czechify '
the Hungarian Slovaks.

" Herr von Labanow (the Russian Ambassador) called on me
to-day officially, and told me that the Russian Government had
succeeded during the last few days in discovering the last three
Nihilist committees and imprisoning all their members. There
was not a single Nihilist left in the whole Russian Empire. And
all connections with the refugee Nihilists abroad were severed.
Tsar Alexander can now quietly return to his capital and reside
there permanently."

I interjected that, while the police were feeling so confident, the Nihilists, some of whom certainly were still at large, would be quietly and safely preparing a new bomb outrage. The Crown Prince answered that he wouldn't bet a farthing on the safety and quietness of Russia.

Then the Crown Prince spoke about Gambetta, and about the possible consequences of his death for Austria and for Europe. He was very much interested and made detailed inquiries about the nature of Gambetta's illness. . . .

" I have accepted for myself and for my wife an invitation to a big ball given by Lloyds at Trieste. Originally it was to take place on the *Berenice*. By the way, the *Berenice* really was damaged by sabotage, and we laughed a lot when we read all the ardent newspaper denials of it. Now, and this is the great surprise, you will learn at *whose* house the Lloyds ball will take place. At the Jew Morpugo's. Just think of the faces that my feudal guests in Prague will make when they learn of our acceptance of this invitation. I must say that the Emperor allowed me to go there without any argument. I attach great importance to this Trieste visit, just because of the Lloyds, who really are of great use to Austria. One cannot quite realize it unless one has travelled around the Eastern parts of the Mediterranean. . . ."

. . . The interview lasted from three o'clock until a few minutes before six. Several times there was a slight knocking at the door, but only shortly before six did the Crown Princess enter the room to summon her husband to dinner. I apologized for the room being full of smoke, but she answered smilingly that she was used to it, from her husband as well as her father.

This interview took place in the small music room of the Erzherzogin (a white enamelled small Boesendorfer piano, a small enamelled writing-desk at the window and white chairs upholstered with light blue silk). When I first arrived at the Crown Prince's private room and we had sat down, the Crown Prince suddenly got up again and, pointing to the left-hand door, said : " I don't trust this door. Let's go into my wife's music room." There we installed ourselves by the desk and smoked continuously. It was a dull December day and it soon became dark. The Crown Prince did not light the candles on the desk until he began to read the letter from Erzherzog Albrecht. When I was leaving, through the Crown Prince's private room through which I had entered, I could not see my way out. A match that I had in my box helped me to find the way.

CHAPTER V

January 2nd, 1883.

We did not enjoy New Year's Eve as we usually do. Father was depressed and worried, because he had news that Gambetta was not likely to live into this year.[1] Unfortunately the news was correct. Gambetta died yesterday. I don't ever remember seeing Father so moved as when he heard about it. Gambetta's death not only meant the loss of a friend, but of a leader of Liberal thought in Europe, and indeed all over the world. We were sitting in the drawing-room after lunch when the news came.

My father said : " So Gambetta was right on the last occasion I spoke to him. He said, ' I wish I could live to see Europe a happy place, but I'm afraid I won't.' He was right, Europe is not a happy place, and it is poorer still for the loss of Gambetta."

He decided straight away to go to Paris for the funeral. . . . Still, Gambetta's death cannot mean the end of all hope for a Franco-Austrian friendship. As long as the Crown Prince lives, and as long as my father works, new links will be forged. . . .

———————

Here are two letters Crown Prince Rudolf wrote to my father about this time.

Prague, January 13th, 1883.

MY DEAR SZEPS,

We have not met now for a fortnight, and much has happened in this time. First of all, many thanks for your letters and best

[1] On November 27th, 1882, Gambetta was wounded whilst examining a revolver. At first the wound seemed slight, but in addition to it he became ill with appendicitis, which led to his death in the night between the last day of 1882 and the first of the new year.

CROWN PRINCE RUDOLF and CROWN PRINCESS STEPHANIE

wishes for the New Year, from the bottom of my heart. May 1883 bring good and rosy days to us. May it strengthen our principles, the principles for which we live, for which we strive and hope. I should have liked to write to you from Budapest, but I knew you were in Paris, and I did not want my letters to lie in Vienna for a long time. By to-morrow you must have returned from a sad, if impressive, ceremony.

The year began under dark auspices. Whatever one may think about Gambetta, a great spirit has disappeared from the scene—one of the first, perhaps the only fighter for freedom of our meagre times. He had the nature of a Titan, an imposing appearance which always filled me with admiration and sympathy. His enemies' exaltation at his death showed that he really did stand up for the principles of Liberalism. . . . You can well imagine the bellowings of pleasure, in all possible keys, to which I have had to listen. . . .

. . . But now, to the point. I must draw your attention to a number of odd things to-day. They are becoming very watchful and suspicious of me, and I see more clearly every day with what a narrow circle of espionage, denunciations and supervision I am surrounded. Be very careful if ever you are asked about your relations with me. Even if you speak to Nehammer, or give him letters or messages, don't omit the slightest precaution. Watch him, too, to see if he commits any solecism; do you absolutely trust Dr. Frischauer?

I have already told you that I had good reasons to believe that our relations were known in high quarters; since then I have proof of it. Futtaky has told me that he was asked by Wodianer a few days ago whether it was true that you came to the Vienna Burg often. Wodianer is a banker, as far as I can gather, the banker of Erzherzog Albrecht—he certainly sees him often. I know only too well the way in which my enemies work. First they send out scouts, then they advance under cover. Then they prepare an ambush by means of cross-examinations, and finally, when everything has been properly prepared, the general attack begins. I have had to go through it all already, in a shameful and unpleasant way. But we will talk about it some other time. The preliminaries are now beginning, the scouting has commenced. . . .

I am sending you enclosed a cutting from a paper, the *Vaterland*, I think. I have received it from the same gentleman[1] whose letter about the Prussian alliance I read to you in Vienna. In a long letter, dated the 5th, which I received in Hungary, he says, after many defamatory remarks about poor Gambetta : " That he owes the fact that he became a dictator at once to his high position as a Freemason, to his Jewish origin, and to his will-power, all of which secured him the allegiance of all Freemasons, all Republicans, all Jews, and all those who do not know how to help themselves. But he always remained a Jew through and through. Nearly destitute in 1870, a year later he was a multi-millionaire, for he gambled and stole whenever he could, and where he missed the opportunity, his friends and protégés seized upon it." And so on and so forth. . . . After some more of these more or less libellous pleasantries came the most interesting sentence, which has been preached again and again by all our short-sighted statesmen : " His death freed Europe from the fate of a Franco-Russian alliance and we must thank God for it. The adoration for Gambetta which practically all Liberal and all the Democratic papers of the monarchy openly proposed, after having published bulletins for months about the state of his health as if he were their monarch, would seem very odd indeed unless one knew that practically all journalists are Jews, christened or unchristened, Jews who stick together all over the world, and who are in addition Freemasons. The rulers of this most dangerous secret society, most dangerous because it is directed against the throne and the church, oblige the world brotherhood to an absolute mutual help, from which none of them can be exempted. Originally, Jews were excluded from it, but nowadays practically all the literate rich are Jews, and zealous Freemasons who are often more numerous in the Lodges than are Christians. But by far the maddest behaviour comes from the

[1] Referring to Erzherzog Albrecht.

52

Wiener Tagblatt, whose editor Szeps " (the epithets I must delete from even the most intimate letter) " was an intimate friend of Gambetta, and called on him in Paris lately.

" Szeps' sadness is certainly frank and justified. I must say that this *Tagblatt* seems to me a dangerous paper, more dangerous even than the *Neue Freie Presse,* because it calls itself a democratic organ and unobtrusively works for the fostering of republican ideas, from time to time disguising its aims by some dynastic, loyal, patriotic leading article, so that it misleads a lot of well-meaning people, and circulates widely amongst the lower classes. Thus, it published recently an article about you which was overflowing with loyalty. It is all very interesting."

Here, you see, we come to the point!

It is followed with a few complimentary remarks about Count Kalnoky. This is the last of them : " His wisdom in speaking and his praiseworthy avoidance, unlike his predecessors, of ' interviews ', is not of course forgiven by the sensational newspapers. . . ."

From these examples you can see their mode of attack, which this time has been a little altered. Previously they began by cursing my acquaintance, as they are cursing you now. This was followed by a few weeks' peace. Then the epistle about the Freemasons arrived, which this time was launched at the start. Then peace again, and after some time the storm breaks. Anonymous letters addressed to me, full of denunciations about the people with whom I am in contact, warnings and cries from the pious and well meaning. Then quite open accusations and denunciations of me in the highest quarters. All that I have been through already. I have been denounced as a Freemason, and complete proofs, with dates, have been supplied, whereas I don't know even the rules of the order.

The source of attack from which the last letter comes is not the only one. There is a big circle and an active committee who are continually brewing complaints and intrigues of this sort.

For a long time they tried to bribe me, but when this did not work, they took to the technique of trying to terrorize me from time to time, and creating many difficulties and unpleasantnesses for me.

So, caution and skill! I may be able to send you during the next few days the plan of a small retaliation; the new organization of the army offers an only too attractive opportunity.

With hearty greetings,

Your faithful RUDOLF.

January 17th, 1883.

MY DEAR SZEPS,

Most hearty thanks for your long and interesting letter, and the enclosures which I am returning herewith. I am not in the least astonished about the intrigues and attacks against your paper, but I think that it would be useful to corner them soon by clever manœuvres.

You should publish that you have learned from well-informed sources that a semi-official paper is going to be started for the sole purpose of damaging the Liberal cause. I think that, after such a notice, no one would buy such a paper, and the whole project would become pointless.

If this statement were not allowed to be published in Vienna, you could give it to Pester Lloyd; it would get known here too, and the Vienna papers could mention it as an unusual report in the Pest papers. You can attribute the story to a remark of a Member of Parliament. However it is done, one thing is certain in my opinion—the necessity of pointing out this cunning manœuvre to the public before they get a chance to be taken in by it. At the present time Government papers cannot do well in Vienna. It is easier to work at Budapest, but even the ultra-official Futtaky is worried, and rather annoyed with certain circles, especially the Minister of Foreign Affairs. I should like to tell you something very interesting, but I shrink from putting it on to paper which, in spite of all our precautions, has to go through the post.

When do we meet again? I'll return here after Berlin,

and as my journey to Trieste and the East will most likely not take place, I shall not be coming to Vienna either. I am sending this letter to Nehammer as usual, but not in the normal way. That is why I think it is better if I don't sign it. I have good reasons to believe that I am under strict observation. An incident with Futtaky, unpleasant for him and for me, proved this a few days ago.

I must finish now. Once more, hearty thanks and many greetings. Yours, 8, 13, 0, 7, y, d.

I'll soon send you the sequel to this magic formula.

CHAPTER VI

DIARY

(Vienna) January 20th, 1883.

. . . Father is being attacked for having attended Gambetta's funeral. He says, and I am sure he is right, that they are some sinister elements in high places (such as Count Taaffe)[1] who are frightened of an Austrian friendship with France because it is a republic.

" No monarchy need be afraid of a republic, provided it is ruled sufficiently well for the majority of its citizens not to want a change. Because if they are well ruled their position is clear and they are free, as individuals." This is what I read the other day.

Still, I'm afraid, because Father's enemies are powerful, and they will try to strike him in the only spot where he is vulnerable—his paper. He has built it up, he has made it into the power that it now is. We all care a great deal for the *Tagblatt*, apart from its political importance, as something which is a part of Father himself.

(Vienna) January 28th.

As we nearly always do, we fetched Father from the office. But to-day will remain in our memory as one of those black days which one never forgets. We were sitting in the carriage when I saw Father coming down the steps looking very pale

[1] Count Eduard Taaffe, Austrian Prime Minister, born 1833, died 1895. The first time Prime Minister from September 1868 until January 1870, then from August 1879 to November 1893. During his second term of office his power was based on the Slav-Clerical majority and he was violently attacked for fourteen years by the Liberal party.

and upset. I knew directly that something serious had happened.

"It is most likely that you are fetching me from my office for the very last time," he said. "The *Tagblatt* has practically ceased to exist. Taaffe has prohibited its distribution by the tobacconists. . . ."

In Austria the sale of newspapers was mainly carried out by the tobacconists' shops, which were licensed to sell papers and stamps. To prohibit the sale of a journal in this way meant that it could only be delivered by post; this in effect was to kill it, as 80% of the newspaper sales were through these shops. This was the intention of Count Taaffe, and, as we learned later, it was instigated by Bismarck, who was afraid of the growing power of my father, of his friendship with Prince Rudolf, of his ideas for lessening Austria's dependence on Germany. This act of brutal force was really illegal, because the paper ought to have been warned first. The situation seemed hopeless, but my father was only depressed for a day, and quickly took up the challenge.

The shares of the company fell to practically zero on the following day; the paper's sales were only a tenth of their usual figure. A stockbroker came to my father and offered to buy up all the shares for a nominal sum, which would again make him the sole owner of the paper, independent of any board of directors of any outside influence. He refused the offer because he did not want to let down the shareholders, who believed in him, and I will never forget the expression on his face when he said, "I will save the *Neues Wiener Tagblatt*." And he did save it.

We went round with him all over the town, renting rooms or shops which were to be used solely for selling the paper. Huge posters were put up outside, saying that here the *Neues Wiener Tagblatt* could be bought. The sales began to go up again, and soon reached their previous figure. Though, of course, the cost was immense.

We decided to celebrate this success with a party and ball, at which my sister and I distributed little dance programmes which were miniature editions of the paper's issue for the 28th of January. This evening was a great triumph, because it was really a political demonstration. All the aristocratic *frondeurs* and many of the politicians who would have liked to have seen the paper abolished were there, and had the dance cards.

Especially significant was the presence of members of the Hungarian Government, who had come from Budapest as a gesture. The Hungarians were strongly Liberal, very much against the present Austrian Government, very much against Bismarck and his Austrian policy. And they liked Prince Rudolf. An interesting light is thrown on this situation by an interview between the Crown Prince and my father at this time.

INTERVIEW WITH THE CROWN PRINCE RUDOLF, *Tuesday, January 30-31, 1883. At the Vienna Hofburg, Midnight*

I have delayed setting down the contents of this interview until February 25th, instead of adopting my usual practice of writing it directly after it took place. I could not find time to write an account immediately afterwards, because of the hectic time I have had since the 28th of January, the day on which the Taaffe Cabinet prohibited a general distribution of the *Tagblatt*. So I am afraid that some details may have escaped my recollection.

On the 30th of January, 1883, Nehammer came to me at six in the evening and said that the Crown Prince had arrived in Vienna from Prague late that afternoon, to be present at the Court Ball, and he had to return to Prague on the following morning. He said that the Crown Prince would like to speak to me, but it would only be possible for us to meet after midnight, when the Emperor had left the ball. If I did not mind that late hour, he had instructions to fetch me from my house at eleven-thirty and take me to the Burg. The many public entrances to the Burg would be crowded then, and so he would have to conduct me through secret corridors.

I heard the chimes at the Franzens Platz ring midnight, followed by those of the Augustinerkirche, as the Crown Prince opened the door. After a short greeting he asked me to follow him. We passed through two or three rooms, then we came into a big room containing an ordinary iron bed and, in the opposite corner, a divan and a table. The Crown Prince was wearing the white dress-uniform of a general, and the Golden Fleece. As we went into the room he said, in a deeply moved voice: "What a dreadful time you've had, my friend. Tell me what those criminals have been doing to you."

We sat down at the table. Nehammer came and laid it for supper with some cold chicken and salad, a glass dish of biscuits and a bottle of champagne in a cooler. I did not accept the Crown Prince's invitation to eat with him, and although he said he was very hungry, he ate very little, but drank four or five glasses of champagne. He was more excited than I have seen him before.

He said: "I have given my opinion about the prohibition of your paper's general distribution, to the Lord Mayor and plenty of other personages who were at the Court Ball. But what's the use of it all. We have embarked on a catastrophic policy, and it seems that no one can alter it now. We are being driven into darkness by Fate, and it's partly the work of the Jesuits, who are closely connected with all the most influential members of the Imperial family. I am not allowed to move, and I have grown so distrustful of everybody around me that life is becoming torture. Soon I won't even trust old Nehammer. And as far as people from the Court are concerned, I dare not speak to anybody who is concerned with Count Taaffe."

I gave the Crown Prince a brief account of the *Tagblatt's* situation since Count Taaffe's prohibition. As our interview had already lasted for more than an hour, I thought that I would terminate it by saying how late it was and that I understood he had to leave early in the morning for Prague. The Crown Prince said, " I am never tired. I never sleep well, especially in Vienna. I always feel better and more at home in Prague than here." And then he began a strange story, sometimes hesitatingly and sometimes hurriedly.

" Two years ago I was in a dreadful situation. There was a kind of conspiracy to make people believe that I had become a member of the Freemasons or some other anti-religious and revolutionary secret society. These accusations grew more and more open, and eventually I had no other choice but to declare —' As an officer I have given a solemn oath not to join any secret society whatever. I am now accused of belonging to such a society. I demand, as I have the right to, the setting up of a military court to investigate these accusations meticulously.' I insisted on this, and the cowards retired, covered in confusion, and ever since they have never dared to utter a word about it again. But do you know who belongs to such a society? Erzherzog Albrecht. That's what is upsetting me so much to-night. The Jesuits founded a union with the aim of Catholicizing Bosnia. They said it was to avoid a schism there." The Crown Prince laughed bitterly. " A schism in purely Mohammedan Bosnia! Well, be that as it may, the Erzherzog Albrecht is, at least nominally, the head of this union, which most likely will bring about serious complications and great dangers for us in the East. In addition, Erzherzog Albrecht is, of course, an officer, and is just as little allowed to belong to any secret society as I am. But it's obvious that whatever the Jesuits want done is permitted."

The Crown Prince continued : " For many months the Hungarians have been very much worried about the turn things are taking. It is the Hungarians who are the only support nowadays for Liberal and constitutional ideas. But they are unable to move. Here, in Vienna, they are afraid of Tisza.[1]

[1] Koloman Tisza, prominent Hungarian Liberal statesman, born 1830, died 1902. Was Hungarian Prime Minister from March 1875 to March 1890.

But his power and influence are limited too. Last summer Tisza, with two of his ministerial colleagues and a third important political personage, who at the time held no official appointment, met and discussed the idea of having me crowned King of Hungary. They took a formal resolution to that effect. Now although there were only four people present at that meeting, Erzherzog Albrecht must have known about it a few weeks later, when he came to me and said, ' Rudolf, I understand they want to crown you King of Hungary. I must warn you against it, Rudolf, because the title of Majesty which you would acquire would only flatter your vanity, but, *au fond*, it would mean nothing. Moreover, if you were crowned, you would have to take a solemn oath to conform with the Hungarian constitution, and then your hands would be tied for ever. Think about your own future and that of our family, and don't take any oath. Don't let yourself be crowned. Don't make any promise. One never knows what might happen, and in certain circumstances such an oath would be an unsurmountable obstacle.' "

The Crown Prince added bitterly, " Since then Tisza is no longer free to make a move. He lives under an incessant threat of blackmail. And naturally, Szeps, you can imagine that there has been no more mention of the possibility of my being crowned King of Hungary."

CHAPTER VII

HERE I shall take the opportunity of saying something about the organization of my father's paper, and some of the people who worked on it, since they are often referred to in my diary.

The offices and printing works of the *Neues Wiener Tagblatt* were situated in an old building : a long passage connected the editorial rooms. In the middle was my father's room. There, every day at three o'clock, the whole staff met; the most important correspondent and the newest reporter were treated alike with the same strict but friendly attention. Moritz Szeps was a leader, but a democratic leader. Sitting in a worn-out old leather armchair, in front of his shabby desk, he would begin to explain the political situation. In turn he would deal with the daily news, the legal reports, the literary and artistic criticism, inviting discussion on each subject. In this way not only did he exchange his own ideas with those of his collaborators, but he gave the whole paper a common style and viewpoint. At the same time he learned to know his staff, by observing their reactions to his review of the contemporary scene.

Amongst the many remarkable people who were working on the *Neues Wiener Tagblatt* in those days, the figure of Dr. Berthold Frischauer, the diplomatic correspondent, stands out. Already he was one of my father's most interesting pupils, and later became one of the great journalists of his time. He had an unequalled genius for striking and following up trails. His gift for piecing together the truth of some hidden political crisis from a few scattered indications, and for scenting the most important news long before anyone else, brought him into the front rank of European journalists. I remember his famous acrobatic masterpiece, when he climbed down the chimney of the fireplace at Skiernevize, where the three Emperors were having a secret interview. From a precarious hiding-place Dr. Frischauer overheard every word and the *Neues Wiener Tagblatt* was the only paper to have a full and verbatim report of it.

Soon afterwards Dr. Frischauer was introduced to the Crown Prince, who at once took a fancy to him; and later he used always to accompany the Prince on his journeys.

Other first-class journalists were the brothers Sigmund and Max S. Sigmund was a writer of charming and amusing short stories and comedies, and was also a dramatic critic; Max, the younger brother, had developed a special line, reporting only dances and social festivities. In Vienna from 1880 to 1900 the carnival played an important role. One society ball followed the other, under the patronage of the Royal Family. Max was the centre of interest, for he distributed the beauty prizes. But besides this he was a real power in the journalistic world. Society women fluttered round him, hoping for a mention in his articles. He was a pioneer of the social columnist of to-day.

Unfortunately both brothers suffered from a serious disease—impecuniosity. Neither of them ever had any money. They always spent twice their income. Sigmund was the happy father of twelve children, who had remarkably healthy appetites, for amongst them they could eat four hundred " *Zwetschkenknödel* " at a sitting. Sigmund regarded his friends as his natural creditors—whenever his purse was empty. And as this was his usual condition, every morning he hired a cab and started on a borrowing tour. He was very particular always to hire a white horse, and whoever saw it stop at his door knew that he would have to hand out ten gulden. No one resented this; he used to ask for it so wittily that it was called Sigmund's entertainment tax.

Max, too, was an artist in borrowing; his medium was letter-writing, and it was impossible to resist his letters. He had not such a high literary standing as his brother, and so did not hire a cab in which to deliver his letters, but modestly sent round a porter with them. There were no telephones in those days, and the post was slower than now, so usually there was a shortage of porters, and to avoid trouble Max kept a porter of his own who took out his letters from morning to night. This man had no fixed salary, he simply received a third of what he brought to his master. Printed on Max's notepaper was the inscription " *L'argent de mes amis est mon argent* ".

Viennese society at this time was at its best. It was full of colourful and light-hearted personalities whose motto was " Live and let live ". Every possibility of a dance or an evening was seized upon. So when my father learned that Constant Coquelin, the leading French actor, was coming to Vienna, he seized on the occasion to strengthen the cultural ties between France and Austria by asking Sigmund S. to write a one-act play for Coquelin to perform with the leading German-speaking actor, Sonnenthal.

The dress rehearsal was made into a great social event and took place in our private theatre. All the leading artists and intellectuals were present, as well as most of Viennese society. At the end Sonnenthal made a speech in perfect French, thanking Coquelin for his friendship. Coquelin wanted to reply in perfect German; the result was indescribably funny, and instead of finishing his speech he embraced Sonnenthal, and everyone cheered.

The day before, the Crown Prince Rudolf wrote to my father: " How I should love to come to your party. But at least I shall be present at the matinée to enjoy this Franco-Austrian fraternization."

DIARY

(Vienna) March 7th.

. . . and Dr. Frischauer introduced me to a very odd young man, who wore an evening dress that was several sizes too big for him. I was surprised to hear he was a professor, he looked too young to be anything so responsible. His name was Professor Emil Zuckerkandl, which I thought very funny. I asked Dr. Frischauer how he could bear to retain such a comical surname. He replied : " You see, he is a very famous anatomist, and at the age of nineteen, before he knew any better, he discovered an entirely unknown bone in the human body, which was promptly christened *Os Zuckerkandl* and immortalized in the medical dictionary. Well, the damage was done; after that he couldn't change his name." He went on to tell me that this young man hated all social functions and seldom attended them. That was the reason for his odd clothes. He did not think it worth while getting evening clothes of his own, so he had borrowed them from the head waiter at his favourite café. Dr. Frischauer also told me that the young professor was famous for playing crazy practical jokes. I could not believe it of such a famous and serious-looking young man and had an irresistible impulse to test him. So later on I suggested to him that, since there were so many top-hats in the cloak-room, it might be fun if we stole them and hung them up on the trees in the park. Of course, I never thought that he would do it, I only said it to see how he would take it. He looked doubtfully at me for a moment, then suddenly grinned broadly and said : " It's a very good idea, a very good idea indeed! Where's the cloak-room? " I could not back out now, since it had been my suggestion. In the end, after heavily bribing the porters, we drove off with a cabful of top-hats, and duly decorated the trees. . . .

In 1883 Georges Clémenceau came for the first time to Vienna, to see my father. He was then forty-six, and had a slim and supple figure, a very interesting and unusual face, with remarkable eyes that were at once burning and cold. He was extremely elegantly dressed, and a man dangerous to women. In the Chamber of Deputies he had already made a reputation for his brilliant scathing speeches—" each word a guillotine ". His career as a breaker of Ministers began at this time.

He came, we saw him, and he conquered us almost at once. He said we must call him Georges and we found him an even better hand at practical jokes than Professor Zuckerkandl. . . .

65   E

(Vienna) June 12th, 1883.

Yesterday we took a trip to Semmering with M. Clémenceau and Emil Frischauer. Emil is a little dull, and I could see that Georges was looking at him in that speculative way in which he always regards possible victims for his practical jokes. However, Georges was tremendously polite to Emil in the train, in fact almost too polite!

As soon as we came to the Semmering and got outside the station, Georges beckoned me to go with him to a little shop, saying impetuously, "I have some shopping to do." So I went with him. "I want a cow bell," he said to the proprietor. "A little one, but of good quality. I'm thinking of taking up farming," he added in a casual voice. Somehow I didn't believe him. "And I would like a small ball of string," he said. "Green string."

We came out of the shop with the bell and the string. He wouldn't say what they were really for, but told me the most fantastic stories of the uses to which he was going to put them.

We soon caught up with the others. Emil Frischauer stopped to speak to the hotel porter, and Georges at once got behind him and fastened the bell to his coat with the green string. Then he began talking to me in a loud voice about the view. Emil turned a little, and, of course, the bell began to ring: he promptly jumped aside to let the imaginary cow pass. But it wasn't there. As he looked round him in all directions for it, the bell kept tinkling vigorously. He couldn't understand it until he saw us roaring with laughter. For some time afterwards he wouldn't speak to us and looked deeply pained. . . .

On the way home Emil lit a big black cigar and hid behind a newspaper. He was still sulking. Georges, who does not like smoking, leaned forward and said : "You know this is not a smoking compartment? "—"Oh, it doesn't matter," E.F. replied. "There is no one here who objects." Whereupon Georges struck a match and nonchalantly set fire to the newspaper.

Now Emil, of course, was too absorbed in his paper to see

what had caused the conflagration, and thought that it was due
to his cigar. So he quickly crumpled up the smouldering paper,
put out the sparks and went on reading and smoking. This time
Georges ran his match all along the bottom edge and the whole
paper burst into flames. Emil threw it and his cigar out of the
window without saying a word. . . .

———————

Georges Clémenceau almost immediately took a great fancy
to my sister Sofie and myself. He was, as he later said, interested in the type of " modern girl " that we represented, and our
interest in and admiration for the arts appealed to him.

He was responsible for my introduction to the impressionists,
at a time when they were almost universally laughed at and
despised. And it was to him, too, that I owed my first introduction to Asiatic art. I think his collection of *netsuke* (these
are beautifully carved buttons worn on Japanese dresses) was
unequalled in Europe. He so loved his favourites that he could
hardly bear to be separated from them. I remember sitting in
our garden with him, when he spoke to me of one of these little
treasures of his.

"You will understand the whole mythology, legend, and
history of Japan if you understand this," he said. "In that
country as in no other perhaps, knowledge and artistic vision
are united into a harmonic entity." And then he told me of
the *netsuke* on which the legend of Ko-Secco was depicted. "He
was a famous scientist of the art of war. He wrote a book about
strategy. The intelligent face of a young man whom he saw on
a bridge impressed him. Ko-Secco took his shoe off and threw
it into the river. The young man jumped in after it. He threw
it twice again, and twice again; without showing any sign of
temper or displeasure, the young man brought back the shoe to
the sage. Then he arranged to meet the young man the following
day. Ko-Secco did not come either on this or on the following
two days. He wanted to test the young man's patience. After
he had proved this to his satisfaction, he gave the young man his

67

book on strategy. When he had studied the book the young man knew so much about war that he became the liberator of Japan from all its enemies."

After a short pause Clémenceau added: "I love this legend because it shows that patience is the genius of all warfare. Even a statesman can win a war and save his country if only he is patient enough."

During this hour in the garden neither of us realized how prophetic his words were.

Not far from Vienna we had a country house—Amalienhof —where we frequently went in the summer of 1883. There were always plenty of visitors when we were there; the majority of these were our Viennese friends, of the "younger set". My father seldom brought his purely political acquaintances down. In fact, the house was for him and my mother a place to rest, and for us a place in which to amuse ourselves. This we did, of course. We rode, swam, went for walks and picnics. Sometimes, too, we would have parties. These were usually very gay. I remember one, however, that seemed to go "flat". The efforts of Girardi (the brilliant comedian, who was a great friend of ours) and myself to brighten it up are described in the following extract from my diary:

DIARY

Amalienhof, July 17th, 1883.

. . . but the party did not seem to be turning out a success. It may have been the thundery weather—I don't know—but people were silent and unsociable. In fact it looked like being a complete failure. I said to Girardi: "This is no good at all. We must do something to brighten them up."

"I have an idea," he said. "Shall we brighten them up by putting them in darkness?"

"What do you mean?" I asked.

"Come with me," he whispered, making a frightfully sinister and conspiratorial face. "Come down to the cellar with me." As we descended, he remarked: "You know I

68

wasn't always on the stage. At one time I did something really useful—I was a plumber's mate. I'll show you how to turn off the gas at the mains. It is an interesting procedure."

This he proceeded to do. The house was plunged into pitch darkness. Sounds of confusion came from upstairs; these were soon reinforced by a series of indescribably frightful howls, yells, and shrieks uttered by Girardi.

Uproar!

When the lights came on again a completely different atmosphere reigned, and everyone was in a good humour. Girardi summed it up by making a horrible pun—" We have lightened their darkness by darkening their lightness."

Amalienhof, July 21st, 1883.

To-day something very nice happened to me. Emil (Zucker-kandl), Girardi, Berthold (Frischauer), and Karlweiss[1] came to my room looking very solemn and grave. " Come with us," said Emil in portentous tones. And they led me to the garden. There I was confronted by a large wooden chair, apparently festooned with flowers. " For a whole year," said Girardi, " you have been very wicked. You turned out the gas at the party, you have done . . . this, that and the other. We have decided that you must expiate your sins. Sit down! " And he pointed to the chair. I sat down. Berthold proceeded to tie me to it. The flowers that were strewn over it were, in fact, strung together on ropes, and it was with these charming bonds that I was secured.

Then Girardi took from his pocket a sheet of paper, upon which was written a poem by Karlweiss, which he read aloud, declaiming the stanzas with tremendous éclat. The poem consisted of a long recital of all my misdeeds for the past year.

When he had finished he turned to Emil and said : " Advance." Emil stepped forward brandishing a long, shining

[1] Karlweiss was a young poet. He, Girardi and Emil Zuckerkandl called themselves my three musketeers.

surgeon's knife. " Are you truly repentant for all your past misdeeds ? " he asked. " I am," I replied. And he severed the ropes with his knife. . . .

(This became a yearly ceremony, I may add. The poems grew better and better. I only regret that I have no copies of them.) ————————

While we were amusing ourselves, enjoying our youth, and gradually growing up, my father and the Crown Prince were seriously troubled about various political developments that were affecting Austria.

The Hungarians were growing more and more restive, as the Croats were tending towards revolt against Hungarian rule, as a result of the Pan-Slavonic idea, which was spreading through all the Balkan peoples. These moves were secretly— or rather, almost openly—supported by Russia, who wanted to acquire an absolute influence in the Balkans.

The Crown Prince had always felt that Austria had a mission to bring European culture to the Balkans. He had hoped that the occupation of Bosnia and Herzegovina in 1878 was the first move towards an " Austrian Expansion to Salonika ". And he was bitter against this Russian manœuvring to prevent the " Peaceful Penetration " of the Balkans.

In many letters to my father he revealed his fixed idea that Austro-Russian conflict in the Balkans would lead to a decisive encounter, which could, as he put it, " end only with a tremendous expansion of Austria, or the downfall of the monarchy ".

Laxenburg, August 29, 1883.

MY DEAR SZEPS,

Many thanks for your letter and your interesting notes. . . . Poor Hungary ! We are facing an epoch-making crisis. Things can't go on like this much longer. This so-called Jew-baiting[1]

—————
[1] In south-west Hungary there was continual Jew-baiting, which at this time began to spread all over the country.

is assuming enormous proportions, and the Croatian business[1] is proof that the Slavonic problem is becoming more and more pressing. Hungary is badly administered, has a bad civil service, no solid basis. It is a country like Russia or Turkey; like these two states it has no well-educated bourgeoisie, but instead many rotten civil servants, Israelites, impoverished peasants, and a disgruntled rabble. The middle-class, which constitutes the true basis of a modern state, is lacking. Such a country cannot emerge victorious from a struggle with Croatia; and there are no sound foundations nor sufficient state power in which to build internal order. Hungary will drift towards complete disintegration, and a time will come when they will find it necessary to interfere from Vienna. But here, where there is this sound basis for the establishment of a modern state, political power is being systematically destroyed by all this " Slavonifying ", so that very soon Austria will be in the same case as Hungary.

Here, however, in addition, there is a reactionary tendency, and personally I prefer the crumbling Hungarian Liberalism to Taaffe's Austria.

Until now Hungary has been our defence against the forces of reaction. If this bulwark were to give way, and Austria under the present regime were to interfere and take the so-called " saving " of Hungary in hand, then we should have to face a revolution for which only ourselves could be blamed —our own well-deserved downfall.

Should I write something about these problems? For instance : 1. The power of the bourgeoisie as the basis of the modern state; how this factor is treated in Austria, and from what elements support can be expected. 2. Hungary as a modern state; its social structure, and the consequences of this. 3. What will happen if the present situation assumes such dimensions that Austria attempts to intervene in Hungarian

[1] On August 15th violent demonstrations took place in Zagrab against the addition of Hungarian official signs to the existing Croatian ones. The army had to intervene and many people were badly injured. This was the beginning of continual unrest in Croatia.

affairs. And *can* Austria intervene successfully under the Taaffe regime. . . .

I think articles on these lines could rouse public attention to the seriousness of the situation.

My father replied to the Crown Prince as follows:

Vienna, August 31st, 1883.

YOUR IMPERIAL HIGHNESS,

Will your Imperial Highness kindly excuse my delay in answering your extremely interesting and important letter of the day before yesterday. The expenditure of nervous energy that the present situation requires, and having spent half the night at the office, makes my handwriting rather illegible, but I cannot possibly dictate such a letter.

There is a note of deep pessimism in Your Highness's last letter, and indeed, an objective view of present events is not likely to produce any other mood. . . . The developments of 1848-49 are repeating themselves, but in a different form. In the case of emergency they rely on the march of German troops to suppress any rebellion against a possible change of the Hungarian constitution. . . .

But I do not give up hope that once more this threatening storm may be calmed. And even if it broke, this ancient state could withstand it, and survive. . . . I put all my hope in the young army, because in it there is a spirit of unity which will bind and hold the state together, even if other ties should loosen or break. The army remains an organized body, in spite of all the disorganization which has taken place in Austria, and which is now taking place in Hungary as well.

And one thing more. As far as I can judge, there is a spirit of liberal education and serious endeavour in our young army which could put an end to reaction if once the government had to rely on armed forces. Your Imperial Highness is quite right; the crisis through which we are passing is an extremely serious and difficult one. But we will overcome it, for nothing can replace this monarchy, it must go on. The breakdown of our monarchy would be the signal for the breakdown of all the neighbouring great states; this is historical logic and therefore a certainty. The time for the end of all European culture is not yet come; our civilization is just at its beginning, as we are only too often reminded.

As for the series of articles that your Imperial Highness was kind enough to suggest to me, the next few days will show whether there is enough time left in which to reason, or whether facts themselves will speak their inexorable language. Let us hope that there will be enough time for reasonable discussion and quiet, dispassionate argument. Then if your Imperial Highness has the time and inclination to undertake the work, I will regard it as a special favour to be able to bring these ideas before a wide public. . . .

Here are two further letters the Crown Prince sent to my father :

Laxenburg, September 19th, 1883.

My dear Szeps,

Many thanks for your letter and the enclosures. It would be very good if I could have a talk with you soon. . . . It is about our Eastern policy. On the 17th I went to Styria with the King of Serbia.[1] I had the chance of talking with him for a considerable time during the train journey as well as while we were driving in the coach, and I found that he knew many things of importance to us.

Following this up, I asked him to come to Laxenburg for a meal on the 18th.

The two of us ate quite alone. I gave him a lot of sparkling burgundy; *in vino veritas!* so he became very talkative and I was able to get many interesting details out of him.

We cannot use all of it journalistically. Much would be

---

[1] King Milan of Serbia stopped in Vienna for a few days on his way to Carlsbad. At that time he was in a very difficult situation because of his conflict with Russia, created by the dismissal of the Russophile Serbian, Metropolitan Michael.

liable to censorship, or too secret. But still there is plenty of material that could be used with effect.

Heartiest greetings from both of us.

Yours,

RUDOLF.

Laxenburg, September 30th, 1883.

MY DEAR SZEPS,

As I have to go with the Emperor to Styria to-morrow morning I cannot see you, though a conversation would have been very useful. King Milan spent the whole of yesterday with me. With the help of some Burgundy I got him talking again. The increasingly precarious state of his country, the situation of the ruler of Bulgaria, and the approaching prospect of the certain downfall of his own kingdom, lend him a somewhat grim humour, and a real gambler's frivolousness.

In Homburg he found more support and received more binding promises than in Vienna. In Prussia this development is regarded more seriously than it is in the rest of Germany; and that is why Prussia is in a much more war-like mood. They anticipate that the situation in the Balkans will soon lead us to decisions which will result in a war with Russia.

In Vienna, i.e. in the Foreign Ministry, the king was received rather coldly, and he was advised not to make such a fuss about his trifling internal difficulties and not to look upon everything so darkly. He was urged to pursue his present political line without provoking a big scandal. That is easily said, thought the poor king, and he explained quite frankly to the Emperor as well as to Count Kalnoky, that there were only two ways left open for him—either to turn round and throw himself into the arms of the Russian Pan-Slavonic policy, or to remain a good Austrian and to take a stand against his own people. But for the latter he would need a concentration of Austrian troops on his frontier. They are very terrified at this prospect.

Only the future will show us whether these prophecies of King Milan will develop into bloody realities.

CHAPTER VIII

THE position now looked so grave that my father thought it advisable to go to Paris, to get an idea of what was happening in France and to discuss the international situation. The following is his own description of that visit.

PARIS. NOVEMBER 1883. IMPRESSION AND INTERVIEWS

Since I was last in the French capital many kinds of changes have taken place. The first thing that strikes one is that liveliness of the streets has greatly diminished. The traffic in the main arteries of Paris has lost its nervous, hurrying character. Theatre audiences are smaller, and many big places of amusement—the skating rink, for instance—have had to close down. The restaurants, which remain open after midnight for theatre-goers, are empty by one o'clock. The big shops, like the Louvre, the Printemps, the Bon Marché, no longer look like fairs. In a word, the town has become quieter and less lively. Is this simply the consequence of the bad state of trade? True, the Bourse has not recovered since the Bontoux affair. True, the French budget has shown a substantial deficit for years, which points to there being a worse deficit in the budget of the French people. The French exports have decreased, while the imports of foreign produce into France have considerably increased. Wages, especially in the towns, have risen, and at the same time the industries of the rest of Europe have so developed that many foreign articles can successfully compete with the French. On the Boulevard des Italiens I have seen in one of the most luxurious shops, letter-paper which I immediately recognized as the produce of the Viennese firm, Theyrer and Hardtmuth, although it was packed in a box with a French name on it. Quite a number of articles from Germany and Austria are beginning to replace French

75

goods, not only on account of their excellence, but also of their cheapness. Strangely enough, this is the case with furniture.

I must mention all this, at least briefly, because this is basis upon which has developed the feelings and moods that I am going to describe.

I

I have been told by an acquaintance of mine at the Foreign Ministry that Fürst Hohenloh, the German Ambassador, said to Minister Challamel-Lacour, on the occasion of the last visit that he paid to him : " I see, with deep regret, a new party developing in France (*une nouvelle couche*) all the partisans of which share the idea of revenge. And this is especially the case in trade and industry, where up to now one found only adherents of peace."

I don't know what Monsieur Challamel-Lacour replied. Anyhow, it cannot be denied the Fürst Hohenloh's observations are fundamentally correct, although his generalization went too far. The process of the change in French public opinion, which at the time of Gambetta's death was not only completely in favour of peace, but even frightened, and one might say cowed, had not reached the point where a war of revenge was desired. This is not the case now, but it might be better to say that this is not *yet* the case. The marked change of opinion in France during the last twelve months is a fact, and it must be of interest to, and worthy of the attention of, all practical politicians. The reasons for this change can best be shown if I put down the facts which made me realize it.

2

I had a long talk with the Duc de Decaces that day after I had arrived in Paris. What this Orleanist leader said about the possibilities of the Orleans cause belongs to a different story. I was struck by the following : " We know that Fürst Bismarck does not wish us (the Orleanists) well. He believes that a

76

monarchist France would be a greater danger to Germany than a Republican France. But the Republic has greatly changed. The epoch of big business, substantial savings, and general rise in the standard of living is over. Now for the reverse—the time of deficits. During the period of the general upward trend, the entire population dreaded war as the worst disturber of their happy estate. It was not the Republic that was the guarantee of peace, it was the good state of business. Now this is over. In its place exhaustion has set in, a deep-seated discontent, serious unrest. And now the prospect of war is regarded with equanimity, and already there are people who say that a complete change of the economic situation can only be brought about by war."

This was all the more astonishing to me in that it came from a man on the extreme right of the Conservative wing. I was inclined to take it as the perfectly comprehensible pessimism of a man who saw no political future for himself or his party. But my surprise increased when on the following day I heard the same type of explanation given by a man on the directly opposite side, one of the leaders of the left wing.

3

The next day I called on M. Clémenceau, and by far the greater part of our two hours conversation was concerned with one theme—war. It was the 14th of November, and I was so impressed by the general opinion that there must be war in the spring, between Austria and Russia, and most likely between Germany and Russia also, that I did not fail to set down Clémenceau's remarks verbatim:

"I recognize the fact that Austria has no other choice than an alliance with Germany. Austria was brought into this position by the mistakes of earlier French policies." After a lengthy historical discussion to prove this, Clémenceau continued: "Emperor Wilhelm obviously wants to end his life in the peaceful recollection of his glorious memories. Bismarck, on the other hand, will regard his work of the unification and consolidation of Germany, and the raising of her to the position of the most powerful state in Europe, as incomplete so long as he has not settled his accounts with Russia. Therefore, he must make war on Russia during his lifetime. The Russians realize this, and they too have their plans for a war. They won't make this war so much with military as with economic forces. At the beginning of the war they'll try their utmost to upset the mobilization in the border provinces by sending in their cavalry on *devastative* expeditions. Then they will avoid any decisive battle, retreat into the interior and destroy whatever they leave behind. What do they care about burning the straw huts of their villages? Thus the war will be drawn out. At the beginning the Tsar will make a solemn oath to his people not to lay down arms for two years, not for a moment to consider the idea of peace, and to share all his people's sufferings. It is believed in St. Petersburg and Moscow that Germany would be exhausted by a war lasting for two years. The conscripted armies of civilized states cannot remain in the field for years without a complete exhaustion of the man-power of those states. It is different with Russia. She has an immense reservoir of man-power, from which can be drawn numerous armies, and economically she has nothing to lose anyhow . . ." Clémenceau stopped, and I interjected the question, "Where will France stand in such a war?"

He answered without a moment's hesitation: "What will France do—there is one certain and definite answer—nobody will hold her back. I won't, certainly. On the contrary, the conscience of the nation will demand a war. This demand will have to be complied with. There will be no holding back. We are not as weak as is thought. We will have clean hands, we don't want our five milliards back, that was a punishment that we had to suffer justly, but we want back what is ours, we want our old frontier lines to be re-established. Even if we were victorious in Berlin itself I would not countenance the demand that a single foot of German soil should be ours.

"Here is what I think about the apparently impending war between Germany and Austria on one side, and Russia on the other. France has no alliance with Russia, and it will not have an alliance with Russia. But the first shot fired in the East must and will call France to arms."

These ideas were brought out by Clémenceau so definitely that I had the impression that he spoke about plans that were already settled, and that he was absolutely determined to prosecute these plans with all his energy and all his power. True, Clémenceau is not in power to-day, and he is far from having a majority in the Chamber. But the excitement that would flare up in France after the first shot had been fired in the East would raise this man to power if the Government did not act as he wanted it to act. The whole situation in France points to a considerable increase of Clémenceau's party at the next general election. He is already one of the most important factors in the country. The opinion that Clémenceau will come to power one day is held generally. It was prophesied by the Duc de Decaces, the Conservative Monarchist; by the Deputies Ribaut and Francis Charmes; by Count Montebello, the "blue" Republican who would possibly agree with a Liberal Constitutional Monarchy; and by Leon See and Tissereine de Bort, statesmen of the Conservative Republican Party.

The "blue" and the Conservative Republicans share Clémenceau's opinions about the next war, although not quite so definitely and emphatically.

4

A few days afterwards I had lunch with Ribot, the leader of the Right-Centre, who, in my opinion, is one of the best informed, most able, and most moderate men in France. There I also met Francis Charmes and Count Montebello, and the next war was always the chief theme of our conversations. These gentlemen unanimously declared that a war in the East would be an immense catastrophe for Europe. They feared that even if Austria secured a military victory it would emerge greatly weakened; and the result would be a profound change in the inner constitution of the Hapsburg monarchy, and a change in its external situation. It seems unnecessary to pursue those gentlemen's ideas, because they were only political fantasies. But they too were quite convinced that it would be practically impossible to hold back France for any length of time once shots had been fired in the East, that the mobilization at least of the French Army would be inevitable. And a mobilized army is like a thundercloud from which lightning is likely to strike at any moment. In the opinion of the above-named people, the French public no longer feared the outbreak of such a conflagration as it did a short time ago. A general " malaise " is about, and war now seems less fearful; the present state of Europe is regarded as precarious, and everyone really wishes for some incident to bring about an alteration in things. Perhaps it would be possible afterwards to reduce armaments and contrive a long period of European peace.

5

In the above I have shown the feelings in different political camps. But what is the position in official France?

My first interview with M. Jules Ferry, directly I arrived in Paris, lasted only for a few minutes because he was busy with his removal to the Foreign Ministry. Later, on October 22nd, I had a conversation with him lasting for several hours. When I mentioned the war danger he said : " A heavy weight has been lifted from my mind, because the complications threatening in the East have either definitely been removed, or postponed for a long time. Emperor Wilhelm communicated directly with the Tsar, who was then in Copenhagen, and negotiated for the withdrawal back to the interior of the Russian troops that had been accumulating in Poland. These negotiations were successful. I have precise information on this point. And look here " (pointing to a heap of documents lying in front of him). " M. Giers s'est soumis completement.

" The retirement of the Russian cavalry from the frontier has already begun. I would have had grave fears if this understanding had not been reached. I can safely guarantee that France does not, in the present situation, dream of an attack, or of a war of revenge. If France were attacked she would defend herself with the courage of despair, and I am convinced that the nation would act splendidly. But Germany need not fear any attack from our side. We are reproached with the fact that certain papers, like the Anti-Prussian, are being sold on the Boulevards, urging a war of revenge. I can only say that neither the Government nor the leading political parties have anything to do with them, and that we believe we know where the money for these rags comes from. They certainly could not exist on their own. They are trying to upset us all the time, they are out to find occasions for reproach. But these tactics, which for quite a long time were effective, now are no longer so. Now we look at such things more temperately and with greater magnanimity. If we are attacked we will try to stand firm. *We* will not attack. The whole situation would be changed if a war in the East took place and its outcome became uncertain. I personally would be against French intervention; I myself would not even order mobilization, but nobody can foretell whether French public opinion might not disregard my views, and demand that we should participate in the war."

CHAPTER IX

AT this time a wave of transcendentalism seemed to pass over the world. It was as if the rationalism of the nineteenth century, and the growth of exact science, had created a reaction against itself. True, this reaction took very material form, and for the time being found its outlet in table-rapping and other drawing-room " occult " amusements. Oddly enough it was " society " which first took to it; and members of the oldest aristocratic families were the most ardent enthusiasts for table-rapping, crystal gazing, and planchette writing; and they all wanted to conjure up the spirits of their ancestors.

———

DIARY

(Vienna) January 20th, 1884.

Father has asked Hansen, the hypnotist, to give a séance at our house. People seem to be very interested in this kind of thing, especially since Charcot began to investigate it scientifically. When Hansen wants to hypnotize anybody he holds a shining crystal in front of their eyes and orders them to fall asleep. Well, he wasn't very lucky with either Sofie or me. He failed completely with us. We were choking with laughter, and poor Hansen was deeply offended. He must have redoubled his energies, for his next victim, Count Zichy, fell into a complete stupor for nearly two hours, from which nothing could wake him. We spent an unpleasant time sprinkling him with cold water, rubbing his ears and feet and holding smelling salts to his nose. Eventually he opened his eyes. . . .

———

The rational mind of the Crown Prince, who had a scientific training and was a student of Leibniz and Descartes, obviously must have been highly critical of this fashionable cult of the supernatural. He and the Erzherzog von Toscana (Johann von Orth as he was known after he had discarded his title) decided to give a lesson to the aristocratic adherents of spiritualism. For many years the Crown Prince had been writing articles for the *Neues Wiener Tagblatt* which, of course, were always anonymous. My father used to copy out these articles in his own hand, at home, so that no one could guess their author. He always returned the originals to the Crown Prince. Szeps was known for skill and wit in circumventing the censor. But his love and admiration for the Crown Prince did not prevent him from altering, or making commissions from these articles, in any places where he thought Rudolf's identity might be revealed.

The Crown Prince himself wrote a description of the " ghost trap " that he and the Erzherzog Johann had devised, and it was published in the paper.

They had been put into contact with a famous medium, known as Bastian, by Baron Lazar Hellenbach, who was well known for his writings in defence and praise of spiritualism. The Baron agreed to put Bastian at their disposal for any investigations and experiments they might like to make.

Three séances were held. At the first two the Crown Prince and the Erzherzog were content to remain simply as spectators. This was in order to remove any suspicions that the medium might have. The ghost trap was set for the third séance, at which were also present five other members of the aristocracy, including Baron Hellenbach.

The séance took place in a dimly lit room, with the seven gentlemen seated round a table holding hands. The medium was in another small room leading out of it. This room was usually separated from the larger one by two sets of folding doors. The outer set had been removed, and a heavy curtain substituted. The inner set of doors was folded back, so that only the curtain separated the medium from the other room. His room was, of course, in complete darkness.

Bastian proceeded to materialize ghosts that appeared and retired, one by one, from behind the curtain. There were tall ghosts and short ghosts, fat ghosts and thin ghosts, six in all. Everyone was duly impressed. It was not easy to produce six ghosts in one evening.

The sixth and last ghost, which was a tall, hazy, female figure, had no sooner floated into the room than the Crown Prince stood up. This was a signal for the Erzherzog to operate the ghost trap, which he did by pulling at a concealed cord.

There were two heavy, dull thuds, and the ghost vanished behind the curtain, which began to sway and tremble in an alarming fashion. Everyone jumped to his feet, the credulous ones in a state of lively alarm at the possibility of some terrifying supernatural occurrence.

However, the Crown Prince and the Erzherzog Johann ran to the agitated curtain, from behind which were proceeding thumping, scuffling and panting noises, and grabbed at it. From its folds materialized the figure of the unfortunate Bastian, in his socks, wrapped in veiling and mysterious paraphernalia.

Even Baron Hellenbach had to admit that his materializations had been very material indeed. But he added, " True, Bastian has been shown up as an impostor. But that doesn't shake my belief in spiritualism in the least. Just because one, or even a dozen mediums are shown up as impostors, it does not follow that all spiritualistic phenomena are false. . . ."

The actual " ghost trap " was really simple, though ingenious. The Crown Prince had called in a clever locksmith, who had fitted concealed springs into the inner set of folding doors. These springs were released by a cord, also concealed, that ran around the wall and terminated beside the seat that the Erzherzog Johann was to occupy. He had but to give a tug at the cord for the doors to slam firmly together, cutting off the ghost from his retreat.

"An ocean of light and progress should pour forth from this town," were the words of the Crown Prince at the time of the opening of the electrical exhibition in Vienna. This summed up much of his attitude to life. Not only the spiritualists had reason to be afraid of light and progress; many leaders of the new parties that had been formed lately in Austria had no use whatever in their programmes for either progress or enlightenment; amongst them were Alfred and Alois, Princes of Lichtenstein, who were two of the most prominent reactionary clericals. They were both tall and exceedingly thin; in addition, they were both blessed with enormous hooked noses. They were known in Vienna as the two Ajaxes. Although they were clerical and reactionary their party had adopted a Socialist-sounding programme, in order to deceive the masses into raising them to power. Alois especially, who was the puppet of forces that sheltered behind his figure, could be regarded as a forerunner of Fascism. For them, Crown Prince Rudolf was the arch-enemy; and at the beginning of 1884 they redoubled their attacks upon him. This time of external and internal difficulty and disorder was very favourable for those who wanted to fish in troubled waters, as can be seen by the following letter from Rudolf to my father.

Vienna, May 17th, 1884.

My dear Szeps,

. . . Nothing but electoral fights and threatening financial catastrophes is arising from the impending disastrous harvest. I fear much bad luck, and plenty of " mornings after ". Foreign affairs are very interesting now. Russia is becoming too strong; England's gradual weakening is unlucky for Europe. I believe that Bismarck's manipulations were not successful this time. Germany will have to bear the consequences in the future. In the last few days they again tried to approach us from Berlin. I am invariably made conscious of these fluctuations by certain private kindnesses. Bismarck is beginning to be aware of Germany's isolated position since the last conference.

I hope to see you again soon. With the most hearty greetings from both of us.

RUDOLF.

A great aid to Bismarck's aim of Austro-German rapprochement was George Ritter von Schoenerer, the founder of the anti-semitic pro-German radical party in Austria, which was also very anti-Hapsburg and pro-Hohenzollern, and whose ultimate aim was the incorporation of the German-speaking provinces of Austria into Germany.

Schoenerer, who was the initiator of the policy of "away from Rome" in the political arena, was an ardent opponent of the brothers Ajax—who were pro-Hapsburg—and their party, which was completely under the influence of the Vatican. But there was one thing that both parties had in common—their hatred and fear of the Liberal Crown Prince and his friend Moritz Szeps. Schoenerer, who was really the most dangerous, was especially eager to attack the Crown Prince, which he did by the means of attacking my father and his paper. My father, of course, did not take this lying down.

DIARY

(Vienna) June 22nd, 1884.

A writ has been issued by Schoenerer, who wants to sue the *Tagblatt* for slander because of the article on his policy. The article really was written by Bechofer, but since my father told him what to write, he will not allow him to take the blame but is going to face the court himself. I think Father is right to fight with all his strength, whenever he can, against this fatal German policy. We have the Crown Prince, of course, entirely on our side, and he is even willing to abandon the secrecy that he has normally to observe.

There is going to be a big fight, but after all, a fight for our convictions is nothing new to us. Father doesn't seem to be worried at all, and we are all busy planning our summer holidays. It will be grand this year; we have been invited to the " Parsifal " festival at Bayreuth. Richard Wagner is grateful to my father, who was fighting for him in the *Tagblatt* at a time when all the other critics were persecuting him. To-day I heard who was the original of Beckmesser in the " Meistersinger ". It is the music critic of the *Neue Freie Presse,* Hanslick, who for years used not only to criticize Wagner but to try and hold him up to scorn, just as Beckmesser does Walther Stolzing in the " Meistersinger."

Bayreuth, July 21st, 1884.

The atmosphere of Bayreuth must affect everybody. Sofie and myself only just dare to breathe, and we feel that we must walk on tiptoe in the sacred precincts of this Temple of Music.

Yesterday's performance was overwhelming. Wagner sat with Frau Cosima in a box. The whole audience rose and bowed to him as if he was a king, and the production itself was too wonderful for me even to attempt to describe it. There is one thing, however, that always strikes me as unpleasant, and that was particularly inappropriate here—that was the *entr'acte*, during which people fought like savages for food and drink. . . .

Bayreuth, July 31st, 1884.

. . . we had been asked to a reception at Wahnfried (Wagner's house). It was given in honour of the marriage of Wagner's daughter. We were also present at the church ceremony. The bride's father was standing near the altar; he wore his legendary short yellow overcoat, and in his hand the " Richard Wagner hat ". He looked very fragile and tired. Next to him was his father-in-law, Liszt, full of life, agile, and upright, despite his age. I shall never forget the moment when I was introduced to him and shook his wonderful, long, nervous hands that had played and written so much beautiful music. . . .

Wagner spoke to me about my father, and how grateful he

was for the way in which he had defended him. " Then nearly everyone was against me," he said. . . .

Wagner was not the only artist whom my father had recognized long before the majority of the critics. Moritz Szeps was a revolutionary in art, sympathetic to every new movement. For instance, when Albert Ilg, Professor of the History of Art, came forward with the discovery that the Baroque *was* art and that it held beauties that the hitherto sacred Renaissance did not comprehend, and was attacked on almost every side, my father got into contact with him. Ilg—this typically Austrian figure of a " revolutionary Hofrat "—began to gather round him a little group who called themselves " Against the Stream ", and from this group came one of the leading movements of the whole European artistic world at that time. I, of course, joined this group, and by now Ilg was my tutor. I shall return again to Ilg, and to this movement which was to be of such importance.

CHAPTER X

No one ever knew for what reasons my father refused to have any notice taken of his fiftieth birthday—November 3rd, 1884. It may have been the result of some premonition that he should not provoke the gods by celebrating this year.

Nevertheless, the Board and staff of the *Tagblatt* disregarded his wish, congratulated him, and gave him presents. The Crown Prince, too, wrote him the following congratulatory letter.

Laxenburg, November 3rd, 1884.

DEAR SZEPS,

First of all, my heartiest congratulations on your fiftieth birthday. May happiness, content, and good health be your lot, and may you have nothing but good fortune with your family and children. These are my wishes for you, as a happy husband and father. But for the man of public affairs, for the true Austrian, I wish for your sake and the sake of all of us, that you should continue with unabated strength as a courageous fighter in the front rank of the forces for real enlightenment, true education, humanity, and liberal progress. Although, at the moment, things seem to be deteriorating; although a step backwards, towards fanaticism and brutality, seems to be bringing us again into a condition that we had long thought to be over and done with; we still believe in a great and happy future, in the final triumph of the principles that we serve—for progress is the law of nature. And you must accept my wishes for to-day, which are not simply addressed to you as a man, but to your spiritual endeavours, as really coming from my heart. Please accept *My Eastern Journey*[1] for your library, and if you occasionally glance at it, think a little of its author and all the ideals for which we have worked in common.

Many thanks for the two letters, which were very interesting, and the books.

Hearty greetings,

RUDOLF.

The Crown Prince's wife also wrote, adding her best wishes.

Laxenburg, November 3rd, 1884.

DEAR MR. SZEPS,

I feel urged to send you my very best wishes for your fiftieth birthday. May nothing but pleasure, happiness, and good health be your lot.

With hearty greetings,

STEPHANIE.

DIARY

(Vienna) November 3rd.

As a surprise for Father's birthday we had prepared a play for him. He knew nothing about it. And we asked him to come into the big drawing-room where it was going to be performed, as if nothing out of the ordinary was to take place. But when he came in and saw what was toward, he was so angry that we abandoned it. . . .

My father's unwillingness to celebrate his fiftieth year was justified by events. This year of his life opened with a series of catastrophes. I will trace their course through extracts from my diary, and letters from the Crown Prince.

[1] The Crown Prince made a journey to the Orient in 1881, about which he wrote the book *My Eastern Journey*.

(Vienna) November 17th.

My father has been sentenced to a month's imprisonment by the jury in the Schoenerer case. Not only is this terrible for him and for us as individuals, it is terrible also for the Liberals, for it shows how the poison of these doctrines is spreading. . . . However, he was not condemned to immediate arrest; he will not go to prison until next autumn. . . .

On hearing the result of the case the Crown Prince wrote as follows :

Laxenburg, November 19th, 1884.

DEAR SZEPS,

. . . I have learned with deep regret the sad fate to which you and your paper have been condemned.

I know your true Austrian patriotism and your noble spirit; and so I know how much more you are hurt by this as a symptom of the sad condition of our country, than by the actual fact of your sentence, which, after all, is a sacrifice that you are making for your beliefs, of which you may well feel proud. In the eyes of all true patriots and all fighters for the cause of modern civilization you have gained the victory of a martyr. . . .

(Vienna) November 21st.

All four of our beloved horses have died from a mysterious illness. It seems to be like pneumonia, but what exactly it is, and what is its origin, no one knows. . . . My parrot—*the* parrot, the best and cleverest talking bird in the world, has also died. We found him stiff and cold at the bottom of his cage yesterday morning.

(Vienna) November 29th.

. . . two days ago I noticed that the leaf-stalks of all the creepers covering our house seemed to be moving; looking closer I saw that they were alive with horrible little maggots busily devouring the stalks. Since then the leaves have all fallen, leaving the house suddenly naked and bare to the cold winds. It is a dreadful sight, horrible, and we have all been very much upset by it.

(Vienna) December 1st.

More misery, more catastrophes. . . . I don't know how to write them down. My dear dog, Foxy, whom I have had for five years, has died of pneumonia. Our old nurse has fallen ill, we think it is with a kind of scarlet fever. And now—but this *must* not become a catastrophe—Ella has got measles. . . .

Ella was our sunshine, our darling. When I was sent to the Tyrol for my health, at the age of seventeen, a nurse was sent with me, and Ella had to come also.

My father had given us enough money for our stay in the Tyrol. I don't know what possessed me to carry off Ella into Italy. But by the time we had reached Venice, our money was all spent, and we had to wire home for more.

I shall never forget our happiness as we drove southwards, Ella sitting on my knee, under the blue Italian skies that grew warmer every day. I don't think that I have ever known such joy and contentment as during those days.

By Christmas of the sad December referred to in my diary, Ella had recovered from measles, and for her convalescence we revisited the Adriatic coast, retracing the steps of our previous journey. And we spent happy days after so much misfortune. But the worst, the most cruel tragedy of all, was yet to come.

At the time we did not know the real nature of the mysterious disease that attacked our parrot, our horses, our dog, our nurse—

our Ella. It was a fatal malady that has only comparatively recently been discovered—psittacosis, parrot disease. And so our poor parrot was the innocent instrument of so much misfortune and tragedy. On the return journey from Italy Ella once more became ill. Again it was with the mysterious disease that was thought to be a form of pneumonia. My father's worst apprehensions were justified. My sister died on the 1st of February, 1885.

Vienna, February 2nd, 1885.

DEAR SZEPS,

My wife and myself send you our heartfelt condolence in this disaster that has overtaken you. I can vividly imagine your dreadful situation, and my only hope is that you will be supported in it by your strong character and iron will. Work will comfort you in your anguish. But this pain must be horrible. The very worst thing that could overtake a happy father. I do not want to go on torturing you with these lines, so I end by repeating my heartfelt share in your sorrows.

Yours,

RUDOLF.

DIARY

February 20th, 1885.

. . . I cannot understand how Father manages to go on with his work in the midst of his sorrow. The moment that *I* take a pen in my hand the picture of Ella appears before my eyes, but *he* does not stop working for a single day. . . . Georges Clémenceau, who wants urgently to talk with him, has asked him to come to Zurich to meet him. I am to go with him, because he has a nervous cramp in his right hand, and cannot write. And he must be able to write, because he expects Clémenceau's statements to be of such importance that they will have to be forwarded to the Crown Prince immediately.

Zurich, March 11th, 1885.

. . . Georges C. (Clémenceau) is really touching in his consideration for Father. He does everything possible to distract him, and the news that he has brought is good. France is now strong and confident, and whoever attacks her must expect a vigorous defence. "And," he said, "I have good reason to believe that there are people who want to attack us. The French Government has received alarming news from Courcelle (the Ambassador). Fürst Bismarck plans to use the present Socialist disorders in Belgium as a pretext for mobilizing German troops on the Belgian border. Bismarck's unusually friendly behaviour towards Russia can only mean that he wants a free hand in the west once more. Such a concentration of troops may easily result in some 'incident' which calls for armed intervention."

Clémenceau discussed with my father what the probable behaviour of Austria would be in such a case.

My father assured him that there would be no likelihood of any Austrian interference of participation in such a situation. And he dispatched a full account of this interview to the Crown Prince. . . .

. . . Georges insists on my father coming to Paris soon, but Father thinks that there is too much for him to do now in Austria to permit him to take any long journeys. He spoke to Georges of the possibilities of a new development in the Eastern political situation—a friendly agreement between Germany, Austria, and Russia. But neither of them really believed that such an understanding could actually be reached.

———

Laxenburg, August 1st, 1885.

DEAR SZEPS,

. . . So the meeting of the Emperors[1] will take place in Moravia by the end of August. But probably no one from Germany will be present. Because of possible Russian attempts

[1] The meeting referred to in this letter was the interview of Kremsier, between Emperor Francis Joseph and the Tsar Alexander III.

of assassination the whole thing will be kept very secret, and even here they are attempting to prevent the slightest leakage of information about it. That's why I should like to ask you not to make use of this news yet.

While the monarchs are embracing each other the Russians will be sending guns and plenty of ammunition to Serbia and Bosnia, to prepare an uprising; it's obvious how useful the policy of our statesmen at the Ballhausplatz[1] has been! I'll send you an article about this, if you want it, during the period of the meeting. I have the whole thing practically worked out in my head already. . . .

_____

DIARY

Vienna, October 26th, 1885.

This is the first time I have written anything since Father went to prison. Of course, it is very sad for us to be parted from him, but really, his imprisonment, instead of being a triumph for Schoenerer, is a triumph for Father. Every day visitors crowd to see him, flowers, fruits, and gifts are sent to him, and even private letters reach him unopened. In fact, he is hardly guarded, or put under any surveillance at all. . . . It was even possible to get a letter from the Crown Prince slipped in to him. . . .

_____

Laxenburg, October 25th, 1885.

Dear Szeps,

Many thanks for your most interesting letter. I am extremely sorry to hear that you are behind the bars. For, in spite of all the special favours that you receive, and in spite of all the philosophical consolations of the " welcome peacefulness " of your surroundings, the confinement is an unpleasant thing—for it has been forced upon you and not chosen by your own free will. My feelings are roused against all compulsion, and I really

[1] The seat of the Austrian Minister of Foreign Affairs.

cannot understand how you can take the thing so calmly.

. . . Our times and manners are becoming savage, there is no doubt about it, and Austria has gone a long way back since we began our parliamentary life. There will soon be sticks and revolvers (in parliament). And what is worst of all, the reactionaries, not excluding those in the highest circles, are exploiting it by saying that people who are not yet even house-trained want to rule, and that they should be properly brought up themselves first before they try to improve the country. That's what they say about the Right and the Left parties, and they thoroughly enjoy the spectacle of Parliamentarianism making itself ridiculous. What saddens me most in this matter is the frightening lack of consideration towards the Germans. True, Knotz[1] and his concerts are dreadful subjects, but a *Germania Irredenta* shouts for help to its brothers in the Reich. Such a complete undermining of the Austrian patriotic feeling among the German Bohemians and among the other Germans in Austria could become very unpleasant in spite of our close alliance with Germany. And how close is this alliance? On this point I have some odd information, about which I would like to speak to you after your monastic retirement is over.

I understand that the King of Spain is not having an easy time. There we will soon have a second European Republic. I am more and more convinced, and this conviction is shared by the Ballplatz (as far as it can be said to have any convictions at all), that Bismarck wants to attack France again. He should be careful. I think contemporary France is much more dangerous than the France of 1870.

To begin a war for no other reason than that the existence of a republic does not suit the Emperor, his Chancellor and a few Prussian Junkers—just to take a little promenade to Paris—is a dangerous move that will recoil upon itself.

[1] The Deputy Knotz, a member of Schoenerer's party, created a violent scene and almost came to blows in the Austrian Parliament, most violently attacking even the existence of an Austrian state; and he stood up for the view that all the Germans of Austria should move for a complete union (Anschluss) with Germany.

The main reason why they want to start a war : . . . They need new glory. Isn't that—except for a few nuances of difference—the same mood that actuated Napoleon III? . . . As far as diplomacy is concerned the time for complete success is at an end. Things have happened that were against Bismarck's will and because of them the magic of his Almightiness has disappeared. . . .

CHAPTER XI

ABOUT this time I became engaged to Emil Zuckerkandl. Though we were very much in love, and though, naturally, I looked forward eagerly to starting our lives together, it was impossible not to feel some regret at the thought that I would be leaving my father, and the interesting work that I was doing for him, especially as my future husband had a professorship at the University of Graz, which meant that I would be cut off from the life and society of Vienna.

The evening my father came out of prison he asked us if our winter clothes were in order, because he wanted to take us to Paris with him the following day. Only Sofie and myself accompanied him, the rest of the family stayed behind.

DIARY

Paris, November 9th, 1885.

. . . Georges obviously regards our arrival as a return for his stay with us in Vienna. He is playing the host marvellously, taking us everywhere; and when he himself hasn't time he makes his brother Paul, who is twenty years younger than him, take his place. Paul Clémenceau is extremely nice, and I believe Sofie has taken a great fancy to him. Besides all this gaiety I have been working hard at the serious business of getting my trousseau together. . . .

Paris, November 14th, 1885.

While Georges was showing me round the Café Anglais, Paul Clémenceau was left alone with Sofie. When we returned they said that they had eaten a " fillipeen ". Georges asked Sofie

Franz Löwy, Paris

BERTA SZEPS

EMIL ZUCKERKANDL

what present she would like if she won. " Your brother," she answered, " has just told me that it is possible to dye red flowers blue. I should like a blue catkin from him if I win."

We all laughed, but the bet was accepted.

To-day Sofie received an enormous basket full of violets, and in the middle was a bright blue catkin. I can't think how Paul managed this. . . .

Paris, November 17th, 1885.

. . . Georges is rather fond of Boulanger, who, according to what Georges says, seems to be a *charmeur*, a marvellous speaker, who wins everybody's heart. If, as Georges expects, Freycinet comes to power soon, he (Georges) would like Boulanger to become Minister of War—and this is the most important Cabinet post so long as Bismarck and his policy remain in power in Germany. My father came in while he was saying this, and Georges turned to him and they began a discussion about the reasons why Austria was keeping to her alliance with Germany —the most generally disliked power in Europe. Georges pointed out that it was really Germany who needed the alliance, and that it was of no use to Austria. Father agreed with this and said that it was perhaps Bismarck's greatest diplomatic triumph that he had brought so many people to believe that the alliance was necessary for Austria. . . .

Vienna, January 12th, 1886.

To-day we arrived home and Father found on his desk a long memorandum from the Crown Prince, which he gave me to read, remarking, with a trace of sadness : " Well, my dear, you won't be acting as my secretary much longer, will you. . . ? "

Because I was struck with the similarity of my father's remarks to Clémenceau in Paris to the Crown Prince's statements, I made a copy of parts of the memorandum that interested me. . . .[1]

---

[1] It was fortunate that I made this copy, because the original was lost, and only a rough draft of it exists.

" . . . Germany needs this alliance more than we do. This is a truth that can easily be proved if one only takes the trouble to study thoroughly the happenings of the last few years. And yet few people realize it, and this is one of the great successes of Bismarck's genius—to isolate Austria more and more from all other powers, and to make it dependent upon the help of Germany. Bismarck taught us to believe that Austria could not exist without an intimate Austro-German alliance; all the same, things in Germany are not going so smoothly as the rest of Europe feels obliged to believe."

A short time afterwards my father received a letter from Berlin, addressed to " the Editor, *Neues Wiener Tagblatt* ".

" You certainly will not mind an old friend of your paper opening his heart to you about the general atmosphere here— the dreadful calm before the storm that seems to reign.

" ' *Bismarck is learning to ride!* ' is the saying that is passed quietly from mouth to mouth. Every afternoon he exercises his old limbs in preparation for the future hardships of a war. I saw him five days ago on the road to Gruenewald, going at a sharp trot, acknowledging the cheering crowd by waving his cuirassier's cap over his head. Intelligent people are growing suspicious of what is happening to Bismarck, who for so many years has absented himself from any public appearances. In all the cafés the gossip of the habitués is of war. People are sick of peace, especially such a heavily-armed peace. Everyone complains of bad times and looks only to war to save things. I have often seen people in the beer-houses toasting each other with ' Long live the war! ' You may be sure that if Bismarck believes the time to be ripe for a war, we will have one. And his Majesty the Emperor of Germany, in spite of his age, would be in the forefront of it. For a Hohenzollern, weakness and age do not exist! And Bismarck believes the time to have come. Every postponement can only mean a setback.

" . . . There are lightning flashes from the East, and we

will soon hear the thunder rolling at our frontiers. You know the favourite month to be chosen for the beginning of a war : It is when the harvest is ripe and there is enough provender for men and horses in the enemy's country. Through all the German provinces and on the Memel ' The Watch on the Rhine ' will sound in July. May God grant that our brothers on the Danube are standing shoulder to shoulder with us. In the meantime the armament factories are working day and night on the new magazine rifles. . . ."

I was married on the 15th of April, 1886. Though we had many presents and congratulations from a huge circle of friends and acquaintances, the wedding ceremony itself was simple, and only our families and a few intimate friends were present, amongst whom was Paul Clémenceau, who came specially from Paris. I insisted on having such a simple wedding because I have always hated the public exhibition of a wedding ceremony, which, after all, is so very much a part of one's private life.

After a short honeymoon in Paris, we returned to Graz, where my husband had to give his university lectures.

DIARY

Graz, May 6th, 1886.

We have come straight home from Paris. From the very first day I saw it I did not care very much for Graz. It is beautifully situated, but the whole atmosphere is that of a little provincial town. We have to live in a flat which is given us by the University. It is in the buildings of the Anatomical Institute. The rooms are very large and my mother has had them beautifully furnished. Emil loves them. But everything here is so different from home that I think it will take me some time to get used to it. . . .

About two in the morning I usually hear the sound of the garden gate being unlocked, and a carriage entering the yard.

I asked Emil what it was and he answered : " Oh, nothing, it's just the stiffs being brought in."

Of course I don't want to bother Emil with all these private little problems, as he is at the moment busy on some research work, which I find excitingly interesting. I love it when he talks to me about it. He is working on the anatomy of the cerebral convolutions. The other day he brought home a model of them, and pointing out some lines he said : " These chiefly develop during the sixth and seventh years. If all parents only knew what a difference it makes to a child whether it learns to read and write at six, when it can be a torture to him, or at seven, when it may be quite easy, they would not boast about their children being precocious."

Professor Virchov, who is by common consent the greatest pathological anatomist alive, has come specially to Graz to talk things over with Emil. He came to lunch. . . . It is odd that such a famous and important man made no impression on me. . . .

Graz, May 15th, 1886.

I have received two beautiful Great Danes for my birthday. I was frightfully pleased with them, but the maids were not so pleased.

I took them out for a walk in the morning, and as the weather was rather rough, I put on some sports clothes that I had bought in Paris. The moment I came into a busy street I saw all the windows open behind me, and women leaned out of them and stared at me as if I was a circus. I could not understand what it was about, and when I came home I asked Emil. He laughed and said that he was pleased that I had upset the Graz bourgeoisie, who did not think it proper for a lady to go walking with two dogs. . . .

I feel that here I am at the North Pole, when I compare the coldness of the people with the warmth of the Viennese.

Graz, June 15th, 1886.

Yesterday Professor Kraft-Ebbing came to lunch. He gave me an inscribed copy of his *Psychopathia Sexualis*, the book that has made him world famous. I like him very much.

In the course of our conversation I mentioned my father's friendship with the Crown Prince Rudolf, and in connection with it, we began to speak of King Ludwig of Bavaria. Kraft-Ebbing is very well informed about him, because the doctor in charge of Ludwig is an intimate friend of his.

" King Ludwig is quite insane," said Kraft-Ebbing, " and I have warned my friend never to trust him so far as to go out for a walk with him unaccompanied by a male nurse. I received a letter from him to-day." And he began to read from it—" ' Dear friend, the King likes me very much, he is extremely friendly with me, and absolutely and entirely under my control. You really need not worry about my safety. . . .' "

Graz, June 17th, 1886.

. . . Yesterday, during a walk in the Royal Park at Munich, King Ludwig attacked his doctor and threw him into the lake. After a struggle in the water they were both drowned. . . .

CHAPTER XII

DIARY

Carlsbad, July 28th, 1886.

I was summoned here (Carlsbad) by a telegram that gave no reason for its urgent demand to " Come at once ". I could not imagine why I was to come, and was rather worried. So when I arrived and found that Sofie had sent for me to be present at the official declaration of her engagement to Paul Clémenceau it was both a relief and a pleasure. I am very pleased. Although I have not really met Paul very many times, I like him very much. He is brilliant, and beautifully bred, a Frenchman *pur sang*.

The Clémenceaus were aristocrats. They did not *lose* their titles during the Revolution, they *gave them up*—because they fought for the Revolution. And ever since then the whole family has been thoroughly and convincedly republican. I am sure Sofie will be very happy with him, though I am sorry that it is her destiny to leave Austria and go so far away. . . . Father regards this marriage as a " destiny " that is rather trying for him, because his daughter is marrying a man whose country is, sooner or later, bound to be at war with Germany. And Germany is our ally. Will it be our " destiny " to keep out of such a war?

It was quite like the old times before my marriage when Father dictated a letter to me for the Crown Prince to-day, telling him of Sofie's engagement, and his own feelings about it. . . .

_____

The following is the Crown Prince's reply to this letter.

104

Laxenburg, August 3rd, 1886.

DEAR SZEPS,

Many thanks for your letter, and most heartiest congratulations on your daughter's engagement, both from Stephanie and myself. But at the same time I must express my sympathy for the great sacrifice that you are making. I can imagine your regret, and I can understand how difficult it must be for you to see your child go from home to a troubled foreign country. Let us hope that the future will dispel your fears and fulfil your happiest expectations. . . .

The very next letter from Rudolf to my father did not, however, give rise to any hope of the fulfilment of my father's " happiest expectations ".

Laxenburg, August 9th, 1886.

. . . Bismarck is afraid of a Franco-Russian Alliance. . . . He is most suspicious of France, carefully watches every movement of General Boulanger, but believes that in his case he is only dealing with a clown.

But the Reichs-Chancellor has even more suspicion of the East than of the West. He has of late been entirely pre-occupied about the possibility of a war with Russia. He talks about it all the time, demands co-ordinated proceedings (with Austria), also on the military side he wants our people to get together with the Prussian general staff, to work out the plans for the mobilization of troops and all war preparations, so that from the Baltic to the Black Sea the army will have a unified and harmonious command. . . .

I understand that Bismarck does not *fear* this war. He is quieter than he was last year, and is much more frank with us, and veers towards a policy that is very favourable for Austria. He speaks mainly about the Russian war—much less about the French. Concerning the latter he always says, in order not to excite the Austrians too much—" I believe that it really ought to be possible to avoid this war altogether—but one has always got to be prepared for it." This gives me the impression that he is soon going to strike. Bismarck says nothing without having a good reason for it.

He now wants to keep the ruler of Bulgaria as an independent sovereign, free from all Russian influence. The same is true of King Milan (of Serbia). He wants to keep Turkey militarily strong because she could be used against Russia one of these days. He has entirely given up his previous idea of dividing the Balkan spheres of influence between us and Russia; he now wants us to be the dominant power there. He is very angry about Italy, and says that in no circumstances should one rely on them; but he will try and render them harmless, or secure them as allies, by making promises to them at the cost of France. . . .

Here is an extract from a letter my father wrote to the Crown Prince on September 23rd, 1886.

. . . it is a fearful time. Are the results of all these powerful alliances, all these intimate friendships, all these confidential talks and conferences nothing but houses of cards that can be brought down by every political breeze? One burning question is being discussed with passionate zeal, both in Austria and Hungary—what has brought it about that Bismarck not only has abandoned us, but has turned round with wide-open arms towards Russia? One feels that old groupings are being dissolved and new constellations formed in their place throughout Europe. But between whom. . . ?

Yesterday I was visited by an intimate friend of Clémenceau and Boulanger, who was passing through Vienna. . . . Briefly, this is what he told me about the situation in France: Boulanger has become a banner around whom everyone in France who has any energy is rallying, though he is a man of only very ordinary quality. The nation is beginning to feel stronger again; they have ceased to be afraid, and have regained confidence in the army. Re-armament is being carried out with the utmost energy. In the next Budget Boulanger intends to demand 400 million francs for the Army Estimates. A third of this sum is for the overhauling of the fortifications and the erection of new forts against possible invasion from the Belgian side. Such members of the present Cabinet as do not appear to be energetic enough may be forced to resign in November—that is, if Boulanger's policy succeeds in the parliamentary struggles, which, in my opinion, is by no means certain.

Georges Clémenceau intends to undertake a journey through Europe before the opening of Parliament. If nothing intervenes he will arrive in Vienna between October 6th and 10th. He wants to observe the situation on the spot. . . .

This is a résumé of the news that was given to me . . . only one more detail about the " re-armament " of France : Boulanger intends to do away with the old straw-filled sacks and to replace them by a new kind of hemp-filled mattress (for the army). This joke costs seven million francs. It is made for the benefit of the common man, to show that he is being looked after. . . .

Ever since the prohibition of the general distribution of the *Neues Wiener Tagblatt* by Count Taaffe, the paper's shareholders and the board of directors had been afraid of some new blow that might be definitely ruinous, and they often tried therefore to moderate my father's policy. They were equally afraid of his strong stand against Schoenerer and of his continual agitation in favour of France and for Franco-Austrian rapprochement.

This tended more and more to handicap my father. The Crown Prince often advised him to fulfil his long-cherished ambition and establish a completely independent paper. Rudolf wrote : " You must found a completely independent paper. You must not be bound by any shareholders or directors. It is necessary for us to have a paper that is absolutely free of any outside influences, that is strong, independent, and unfettered. Together, we can create a new Austria. We cannot and must not allow Austria to be taken in tow by Germany. Republican France should take the place of reactionary Prussia in our foreign relations. *Look towards the West*—that should be our programme!

DIARY

Graz, October 5th.

I was worried by the letter that came from Father to-day, although I can perfectly understand and sympathize with his decision. He has completely made up his mind now about the *Neues Wiener Tagblatt*; he is going to leave it and establish a new paper of his own, which will be called the *Wiener Tagblatt*.

The Crown Prince met the French financier, Baron Hirsh, at a shooting party, and introduced him to my father. Hirsh has now put sufficient money at Father's disposal to enable him to start the new paper. Father, who always likes to strike while the iron is hot, decided that the first number should be published by the autumn. Though it means that he is throwing away a safe income and an assured position to embark on a risky new adventure, he will be happy to be able to defend his convictions and fight for his ideals without outside interferences and the limitations that have been imposed upon him by shareholders and boards of directors. I do hope he will succeed with this new paper. It means so much to him personally, and that makes it important for all of us. . . . I am glad that Sofie's approaching wedding makes it necessary for me to go to Vienna in any case. Now it is possible for me to be with him during the first weeks of the new venture. . . .

Vienna, December 23rd.

Yesterday Sofie was married to Paul. . . .

Georges C. (Clémenceau) was one of the witnesses. In spite of

Sofie's happiness, and in spite of our deep attachment to Paul, we were all a little depressed at the idea of her going to live so far away from us.

. . . While we were at dinner—it was quite a small family party—and I was sitting between Georges and Albert Clémenceau, the butler came in and said that someone wanted to speak to me—" the gentleman who used to be your masseur," he said. " He says that it is most urgent."

I went out after the coffee was served, and found old Nehammer waiting. The Crown Prince had sent him to ask if it was possible for Georges and my father to see him that night. They would have to visit him at midnight; the Crown Prince apologized for suggesting such a late and unusual hour, but said it was the only time when they would be secure from interruption. Nehammer said that, if it was possible for them to come, he would wait for them at the steps, where he usually arranged to meet my father for these interviews. . . .

———————

All the existing biographies of the Crown Prince Rudolf are doubtful whether this interview between Rudolf, Moritz Szeps and Clémenceau actually took place. While I knew that it had, I knew no details of the talk, and did not realize that my father had made a record of it. In searching amongst my father's papers, however, after his death, I found some rough notes of this interview. I could find no final or worked-out version of the notes, and I believe that my father, contrary to his usual practice, did not make such a version. That probably is why only the remarks of the Crown Prince and of Clémenceau are noted, and his own remarks are omitted. However, his omission to make a full record of such an important interview may have been due to nothing more significant than his personal preoccupations at the time, with Sofie's wedding, and the organization of the new paper.

I reproduce the notes below.

INTERVIEW WITH THE CROWN PRINCE AND GEORGES CLÉMENCEAU on the night of December 22-23, 1886

The Crown Prince greeted Clémenceau very warmly. "I have wanted to meet you for a long time, knowing you to be such a real friend of Austria. I shall never forget the words that you addressed to Mr. Szeps years ago—'France would rather go to war than allow the German Provinces of Austria to become incorporated into the Reich.'"

CLÉMENCEAU: "Quite apart from the warm feelings for Austria that I personally entertain—and I would not allow my feelings to interfere with any policy that I was pursuing for the good of my country—I have always wanted a free and independent Austria because it *is* for the good of my country. In fact, Austria's freedom is an absolutely vital necessity for France in order to counterbalance Bismarck."

THE CROWN PRINCE: "Germany has never been able to realize the enormous value and significance of having German, Croatian, Polish and Hungarian peoples grouped around one throne. Our Hapsburg state has actually long since put into practice, in a miniature form, Victor Hugo's dream of a 'United States of Europe'. Austria is a bloc of different nations and different races under a united rule. At least, that is the basic *idea* of Austria, and it is an idea of enormous importance to the civilization of the world. Because the present execution of this idea is, to put it diplomatically, not altogether harmonious, it does not mean that the idea itself is wrong. It only means that such an idea requires a liberal rule for its harmonious and balanced execution. . . . This is one of the main reasons why, in my opinion, Austria should co-operate with the Western democracies. It is among them that the real liberalism that we require—personal freedom and the absence of racial hatred and dissension—can be found."

CLÉMENCEAU: "The qualities of which you speak are those which Bismarck would list under the head of 'weaknesses'. Bismarck certainly is a genius, but he has never succeeded in taming the Prussian Junker in himself. His policy towards

Austria seems incomprehensible. Why did he intend to offer France Metz and Lorraine against the German-speaking provinces of Austria, when it must have been in his interest to have a strong Austria for his ally? On the other hand, why does he try with all his force to entangle Austria in this mad Eastern policy?"

THE CROWN PRINCE: "Our Balkan policy! This is a mission which, alas, is often misunderstood in France and in England. It is our noblest mission to bring enlightenment and civilization to the East. You in France do not realize what work has been done for Bosnia during the past eighteen years, since its occupation—the occupation that is still begrudged by France and England! It is one of my greatest dreams to fulfil what I call the ' penetration pacifique' of the Balkans. Only Russia bars the way, drunken, threatening Russia, who means to keep the Balkan peoples imprisoned in barbarism and darkness, and to use them as a threat against us whenever she pleases."

CLÉMENCEAU: " Here again, a real understanding with us and with England can only bear good fruit. What prevents England from agreeing with your Balkan policy? It is that they feel indirectly threatened by Germany. An intimate Austro-German alliance, extending from the North Sea and the Baltic to the Mediterranean and the Black Sea seems to them only to strengthen the German threat."

THE CROWN PRINCE: " The Prince of Wales is friendly to me. We see each other whenever he comes to Austria, and I am quite positive that when we both come to the throne England and Austria will be able to come to a complete agreement. I only wish that our discussion to-night could lead to collaboration and harmonious understanding between our three countries."

Clémenceau departed, after shaking hands with the Crown Prince, most favourably impressed by him.

CHAPTER XIII

DURING the next few years I lived in a kind of backwater at Graz, away from the confused and turbulent currents of European affairs that ran through Berlin, Paris and Vienna. And since I was no longer in daily touch with my father's work, I shall have to rely for the story of those years chiefly on my memory, with the briefest references to contemporary letters and documents.

The year 1887 was marked by continuous and disturbing changes in German policy. With one hand they were continually making advances to Austria, the other they stretched out in seeming friendship to Russia.

These manœuvres began to have an upsetting effect upon the Crown Prince. As his letters and interviews have shown, the Balkans were his main preoccupation, and it is not too much to say that his concern for what he considered as Austria's civilizing mission there was one of the prime motives of his life. And Germany's alternating political flirtations, now with Austria, now with Russia, almost reduced the Balkan situation to a state of chaos. Rudolf was reduced to a condition of nervousness and despair.

A letter from my father to the Crown Prince gives some idea of these fluctuations of German policy.

January, 1888.

. . . to-day it seems that Bismarck has won over the Tsar, or at any rate has at least quietened him down. Once more one of these astounding alterations in the situation has taken place. . . . It is necessary to read to-day's *Norddeutsche Zeitung* to get an idea of this game of sudden changes that they are playing in Berlin—at our expense. One day they sound the alarm!

Everyone must be in readiness; they rave because military pre-parations are not moving quickly enough. The next day they begin malicious reproaches to the effect that we (Austria) our-selves are responsible for this alarm, and advise us to go home peacefully and quietly. . . . All this is bound to have a bad ending. And, in addition, they behave in Berlin as if they were saving us regularly once a fortnight. In reality, of course, it is no one but Germany who is threatened. . . .

It had been Bismarck's aim for some time to bring about a semblance of friendship between Rudolf and the son of the German Crown Prince Wilhelm, who was about the same age as he was. This would help, though but superficially, to give an appearance of good relations between the two countries. But he was not able to bring this about. Prince Wilhelm declared quite openly, " I know the very idea of anything Prussian is hated by Rudolf." And Rudolf remarked to F. M. L. Latour : " Believe me, it really is no pleasure for me to have to meet this dyed-in-the-wool reactionary and Junker ! "

One of the reasons for Prince Wilhelm's antipathy to Rudolf was jealousy of the good understanding that prevailed between his parents—with whom he himself was on bad terms—and Rudolf. Rudolf became increasingly friendly with the German Crown Prince Friedrich and his wife Victoria (a daughter of Queen Victoria). In Friedrich Rudolf recognized something of a kindred spirit, a man with the same Liberal ideas and ideals as himself. The future political possibilities of such a friendship between the German and Austrian heirs apparent were infuriat-ing to the reactionary Wilhelm, and also to the ruling powers of both countries, who were certainly alive to all the potentialities of such a situation. Indeed, it became a source of diplomatic anxiety, and the Austrian Ambassador at Berlin even wrote to Rudolf : " The association that you had here (in Berlin) with the Crown Prince and Princess, has been observed, and made the subject of pointed comment. It is asked—Does this not signify some 'cooling off' in your friendship for the Prince William?"

"There is no 'cooling off' possible, for the temperature of our relationship has always been at absolute zero," Rudolf remarked in a conversation that my father noted down. In these rough notes my father also remarked that the Crown Prince seemed to him to be getting more and more nervous and upset. The strain of the political situation, added to his private worries, and the incessant intrigue, surveillance, and espionage with which he was surrounded, was affecting his whole demeanour.

The following incident appears significant in the light of later happenings. During a visit of my husband to Vienna, Emil met the Crown Prince, who asked him whether he did not find it gruesome to live in the Anatomical Institute, surrounded with corpses and skeletons, and an atmosphere of death. "No," answered my husband, "even skulls present certain beauties. And one gets used to that idea that death is not a misfortune but a necessary, even miraculous, fulfilment of life." The Crown Prince seemed to be struck by this idea, and said in a very determined way, "One should face the idea of death straightforwardly." And he asked my husband if he could let him have a skull. This, of course, my husband did, and sent him a specially prepared and polished specimen, which Rudolf kept on his desk for the rest of his life.

To speak the language of the psychologists, this might be taken as a symbol of a subconscious death-wish on the part of the Crown Prince.

The old Emperor Wilhelm of Germany died on March 9th, 1888. Friedrich's ascent to the throne would, it seemed then, mean a considerable change in German policy, a change in the direction of liberalism, a turning towards the western and progressive states, and away from Russia. The year before (1887) a secret Russo-German "neutrality pact" had been signed, guaranteeing that if either of the two powers were attacked by a third, the other would remain "benevolently neutral". This pact, of which Austria was not officially informed, appeared to set the seal upon Germany's friendship with Russia, and—this was what particularly upset Rudolf—to give her practically a free hand in the Balkans.

Already, after a month of Friedrich's reign, this friendship with Russia seemed to be weakening. Alas! on June 15th, 1888, only three months after he came to the throne, Friedrich died, and was succeeded by Wilhelm.

Once more a change in German policy! Once more danger to Rudolf's Balkan ideals! Not only was there a return to the strain of the previous year, but that strain was intensified, for now the death of Friedrich had quashed all hope of better things. So felt Rudolf on the eve of his thirtieth birthday. My father wrote him the following letter.

(undated)

. . . not to become slack during times of inaction, to keep body and spirit strong in preparation for times of activity—this is the task that your Imperial Highness has set yourself; and it is being fulfilled by you daily. . . . You have not grown slack when so many grew slack, not given in to what was apparently unchangeable. And because the Crown Prince does not slacken, we all keep up our hopes for the future of a great, glorious, free and wealthy Austria. . . . In the course of the past year you have had to put up with much malice, much knavery; but you have withstood it all, with admirable sang-froid. They know that you desire great ends, that you are able to perform great deeds—and those who don't know it feel it. That is why you are being fought with such unusual weapons. You have many antagonists and enemies who try to bar your intended course. But you have counted on your-self, on your own genius, on your strength and powers of endurance. And you are right to count upon all this. You must add a little luck to it—not necessarily as much as your true friends and admirers wish for you—but just a *little* luck, and then you will achieve greatness for this Monarchy which is our fatherland, greatness for your own glory, and for the glory of the people of Austria who depend upon you. . . .

To this letter Rudolf replied :

Laxenburg, August 21st, 1888.

DEAR SZEPS,

Many thanks for your letter, and the good wishes that speak so warmly to the heart, since they come from a faithful soul.

The age of thirty marks a dividing point in life, and one that is not too pleasant either. Much time has passed, spent more or less usefully, but empty as far as real acts and successes are concerned. We are living in a time of slow, drawn-out rottenness, and no one knows for how long we are to continue in this way. And each year makes me older, less fresh, and less efficient. The necessary daily routine is, in the long run, very tiring. And this eternal preparing of oneself, this constant waiting for great times of reform, wears out one's creative power. If the hopes and expectations that you are placing in me are ever to be realized, a time of war must come soon, a great time in which we will be happy, since after its glorious end we could build the foundations of a great and peaceful Austria.

A lifetime that is spent in ceaseless movement, often, in fact usually, exhausted and strained by manifold activities, is short when one measures it in terms of real spiritual activity. However, be that as it may, one must believe in the future. I hope and count on the next ten years.

With hearty greetings,

YOUR FAITHFUL RUDOLF.

At the age of thirty Rudolf was faced with a strengthening of all the forces that were opposed both to his ideals and himself. Between his own father and himself there was an increasing tension. The new German Emperor became more and more openly unfriendly to Austria. Even the Emperor

Francis Joseph lost patience when Wilhelm suddenly made a long pro-Russian speech. He had something of a revenge when the Kaiser visited Vienna, in October 1888, and was given a noticeably cool reception by the population. In a letter dated November 3rd, my father wrote to the Crown Prince—" It was a beautiful, really Austrian occasion. One could see that Vienna does not like the Emperor Wilhelm.

" I have heard several people remark how odd it was that the Emperor Wilhelm came straight from Stuttgart and Munich to Vienna, as if he was, so to speak, ' continuing ' his tour of the Southern German courts. . . ."

And so the year 1888, " a time of slow, drawn-out rottenness " came to its end. A letter of my father's to the Crown Prince, written at the beginning of the new year, expressed something of their hopes and fears for 1889, that was destined to see the tragic ending of all Rudolf's hopes and fears.

Vienna, January 1st, 1889.

Your Imperial Highness,

" This peace is ominous "—so your Imperial Highness writes in your last letter—" like the calm before the storm."

The past year will figure in history as one of *pompe-funèbre*. It was no more than that. But, in certain circumstances, even that is enough. Because, when that which is rotting, faded and old, gives way to that which is fresh and young, what really is an act of renewal and rejuvenation takes place, which is necessary for the world. But the *pompes-funèbres* of the year 1888 did not renew and rejuvenate very much. And the peace that is hanging over Europe is really ominous.

What will develop out of it?

The old man in Friedrichsruh does not need a new epoch. He has made immense achievements—he can win no more— he can only lose. He knows that, and that is why he will do everything to prevent the outbreak of a great European conflict.

Metternich behaved in the same way, in order to preserve his peace. Metternich, too, from the same fear, bequeathed decisions and solutions to the future that he should have tackled himself. And the end was the great breakdown, through the revolution. Is not Bismarck's policy preparing a revolution in Germany?

In Berlin they are afraid of revolution, afraid of France, and they even seem to be afraid of Crispi.

This storm cloud cannot hang for ever. The year of change must come some time. Will it be the year 1889? The signs do not appear to make it seem likely. God knows what might have happened if the French had not held their International Exhibition. The French have ceased to be afraid of Germany —and this is an important sign of the times! But the International Exhibition means peace in France. . . .

The French will most likely be successful in contriving that the Exhibition passes peacefully—and so the year 1889 will remain very close and sultry, unless a sudden flash of lightning strikes and the storm bursts upon us. . . .

EPILOGUE TO THE FIRST PART

As the preceding pages have dealt so much with the Crown Prince, his political views and struggles, and his truly friendly interest in my father, I think it justified that I should end this part of my reminiscences with a brief account of Rudolf and Mary Vetsera, since it was with her that Rudolf was united in death on January 31st, 1889.

At the time when the Crown Prince was still residing at Prague, he paid an official visit to the " ghetto ", the Jewish quarter there. During this visit he met a young Jewish girl of great beauty. They fell in love one with the other. Her parents, however, made it impossible for them to meet, by hiding her away in the country. But in the hope of seeing her beloved once again she ran away, and secretly returned to Prague, where she fell ill of fever on the day of her arrival, and subsequently died.

Ever since then the Crown Prince had often visited the Jewish cemetery secretly at night, bringing flowers to place on her grave. He could not forget her. And it was not until he met Mary Vetsera that passion re-entered his life.

They met three months before their death. Rudolf wanted to get a divorce from his wife, the Crown Princess Stephanie, in order to marry Mary Vetsera. But he knew that his father would accept no authority other than that of the Pope for divorce. So he wrote to the Pope, confessing his love, and imploring him to intercede with his father.

The Pope merely sent the letter on to Francis Joseph, advising him not to give in to his son's folly.

On the day that the Emperor received the Pope's letter, Prince Reuss, the German Ambassador, held a reception, to which the Emperor was going. The Crown Prince was also to be present.

The whole Court and aristocracy were standing in a circle awaiting the arrival of the Emperor. When he entered the ballroom he walked round the circle, stopping with each person for a moment and speaking a few words in greeting. But when he came to the Crown Prince, who bowed deeply, the Emperor abruptly turned his back on him. A shudder of horror ran through the guests. The Crown Prince halted for a moment, as if he had been struck, then left the room.

The same evening he asked my father to call on him. My father found him in a dreadful state of nervous excitation. Again and again he repeated, " The Emperor has openly affronted and degraded me. From now all ties between us are broken. From now I am free! "

The Crown Prince had met Mary Vetsera on November 5th, 1888. She was only seventeen at the time. Her mother came of a very old Greek family, and from her she had inherited an almost oriental grace of demeanour. It has been said that she very much resembled the Jewish girl whom Rudolf had loved before. She was a charming, flower-like creature. It is enough to quote a few of her letters to show the ecstatic happiness and despair of this young girl's passion, so tragically brief.

She writes to a friend :

" I have two friends, you and Marie Larich. You work for my soul's happiness, and Marie for its downfall. . . ."

The friend implored her to give up her love, but pleas were unavailing. Mary writes :

" To-day you will have a happy letter, for I was with him. Marie Larich took me with her shopping, and then to be photographed—for *him*, of course. Then we went to the Grand Hotel, where Bratfisch, his coachman, was waiting for us. And then, at a gallop, to the Burg. An old servant was

PART II

CHAPTER I

In the summer of 1888 Emil Zuckerkandl was unanimously elected Professor of Anatomy at the medical school of the Vienna University.

At that time the medical faculty of Vienna University comprised an assembly of genius. There was Bilroth, who only a short time ago had performed what then had seemed an absolute miracle—the resection of the stomach. There was Albert, the forensic genius. There was Nothnagel, the great physician, who laid down the fundamental rules of modern medicine, and originated the saying—to which he himself lived up—" A good doctor must be a good man ". There was Meynert, the most famous anatomist of the brain who has ever lived. Each in his own line was unequalled in importance and ability in medical history.

Another of the great men who had been reared at the Vienna medical school, and who became a friend of ours, was Wagner-Jauregg. He had spent a considerable part of his life in Styria, the district that, above all the other Alpine countries, had the highest percentage of imbeciles and idiots. They looked like the horrible and fantastic dwarfs of fairy stories; their enormous heads lolled above undeveloped bodies that were carried on weak, often crippled legs. Wagner-Jauregg began to cure this disease—the result of abnormal functioning of the thyroid gland—with iodine salts. When he first stated his theory a storm of disbelief was raised amongst his brother-scientists, but his treatment worked, and it is owing to him that to-day the population of this district is almost completely normal.

But it was also Wagner-Jauregg's destiny to find another

epoch-making cure for a disease to which the human race is prone. I can remember my husband's passionate interest in this work of Wagner-Jauregg's, which he carried on for years. He, as the head of the clinic for nervous diseases, was continually being confronted with cases of general paralysis of the insane. No one was cured of it—unless they also contracted some other disease which was accompanied by a high fever. Then they seemed to recover from the paralysis. Wagner-Jauregg observed this apparent coincidence, and came to the conclusion that it was not a coincidence at all. He began to work on the problem, and his researches led him to the discovery that very high fevers can kill the spirochætes in the organism that produces this form of paralysis. The next question was—how to produce such a high fever, which also had to be recurrent. In the end he solved the problem with almost melodramatic brilliance, by giving his patients carefully regulated attacks of malaria.

Another research worker of that period whom I often used to meet, was Steinach. This young scientist had opened up an entirely new field of research—the physiological states associated with the process of ageing. This problem, of course, besides being of enormous general scientific interest, touched upon one of the eternal hopes and dreams of humanity—rejuvenation and perpetual youth! Steinach's great achievement was, technically, the transplantation of glands, and his ideas and his technique opened up a whole new field of knowledge, which has led to the miraculous discoveries of the work and functioning of the ductless glands in the human body.

It is pleasant for me to ponder over my memories of all these great men of science whose work at the Vienna medical faculty was playing such a leading part in the great international field of scientific progress, and who were united in friendship, as in their common aim. In the midst of them all moved the figure of my husband, in whose studies they were all deeply interested, and to whose personality they were all drawn. In him was incarnated what I regarded then, and still regard now, as the pure, almost fanatical spirit of science. But instead of being led by his single-minded devotedness into the eccentricities and oddnesses characteristic of so many great men of science, he retained a singular balance of character. An unfailing humour, an exuberance of artistic sensibility, a warm and tender love for the common people, made him beloved by everyone.

Until he was sixteen Emil Zuckerkandl believed that he would become a virtuoso of the violin. His great musical gifts seemed to predestine him to a musical career, and when he was still a small child it was decided that he should become a violinist. He never attended the ordinary schools—he had no time for any education that was not musical. But one day he finished his practice, put his violin aside, and said: " I am going to *learn*."

He shut himself up in his room and began to read, and read, and read. . . . In one year, by himself, he covered and mastered all the groundwork of ordinary education that he had missed, and at the end of this period he passed the university entrance examination.

He attended the classes of the great anatomist Hyrtl, a man much beloved, much feared, hard to approach, but a great teacher and tutor.

Hyrtl had an old laboratory assistant called Herusch, who, as he was never tired of pointing out, was the only man unafraid of the Professor, and for this reason much respected by the students. To the Professor there came old Herusch one day, bearing a beautiful preparation of the nerves of the knee articulation. The following story was well known in the University. " Look here, Professor," he said. " Here is some pretty fair work for a change."

" Hm," answered Hyrtl sceptically, and then, after having given a glance at the preparation, " Hm, yes, not bad at all. This chap understands his work better than most of his fellow butcher's assistants. What year? "

" No, Professor, no," answered Herusch triumphantly. " He is quite new, in his first term, an odd one, very slim, almost a little boy."

The surprise was a success. Hyrtl asked the young man with the peculiar name to be brought to him. In an unusually short time Hyrtl made him a demonstrator, and not long afterwards he discovered the hitherto unknown bone which was named after him—*os Zuckerkandl*.

Still, his brother was not satisfied with him. True, Zuckerkandl had forgotten to apply for his Fellowship, but the reproach of his brother, " You'll never make a career—no one ever succeeds in making a career who does not care about it! " did not come true. Zuckerkandl became one of the youngest professors the University had ever had, although he had never been a Fellow at all.

No, Emil Zuckerkandl never had time to bother about a " career ". He was much too busy with his work, with his researches on the structure of the human brain, on the anatomy of the nose and throat and teeth—all fields whose details were practically unknown at this time, so that his discoveries in them became the foundation of the work of modern surgical specialists.

Then for a time an odd change seemed to come over my husband. It was as if he had almost forgotten the existence of his little son and his wife. Nothing appeared to touch him or move him in the least. This was not depressing or offensive to me and his friends. It was as if he had just forgotten about the ground on which he trod and had risen to a state of higher consciousness.

This went on for some time and passed away only after he had finished the work he was engaged on at the time—his greatest and most important discovery, that of the *chromafine system*, " a form of tissue that has ' wandered out ' from the central nervous system, and which is of great importance in determining and maintaining the whole blood pressure of the human body," as he explained it to me.

His story of how he had come to make the discovery was characteristic. He said that it was due to his being short-sighted, which had made him notice minute variations in the structure of the kidneys and the tissue surrounding them.

But my husband never made any money beyond his rather small salary. He never troubled to arrange proper contracts for his books, which sold and are still selling in thousands. They benefited science and humanity—never himself. To a young woman who had been accustomed to comparative luxury, our standard of living seemed rather low, and sometimes I could not help sighing over it.

"Now come," my husband said. "Don't be so unphilosophical. If I had to plan and think out ways of making money from my writing, then I couldn't possibly be able to plan and think out what to write."

So I gradually learned to think how best to save money and to economize. I had to find a house for us in Vienna when my husband got his professorship, and it had been worrying me for some time, because it was hard to find something suitable both to my taste and our pocket. Then one night I had a dream that, after a long search, I had found a house, a wonderful house. It was in a street called " Nusswald ", which I had never seen or heard of before. It was a beautiful old house with large rooms. I remember passing through them in my dream and then going out of the hall into a big garden in which there was an absolutely magnificent, smooth and ancient lawn, bordered by tall walnut trees. How I regretted it when I woke up and found myself in our temporary home with yet another day of house-hunting lying ahead of me!

The first place I was going to was rather distant, and when I gave the cabman the address he asked me if I would prefer to go there direct by a route that was rather unpleasant, or to go by a slightly longer way which, he said, was very pretty. I did not know this pretty route, and being in an exploratory mood, I decided on it.

We had not been fifteen minutes on our way when we came to a street that looked strangely familiar. I could not think why, because I was certain that I had never been in this part of the town before. I asked the cabman the name of the street. " Nusswald," he said, and to my amazement, as I looked out of the

window, I saw the house, the wonderful house that I had
dreamed about.

It bore no sign to show that it was to let, but excitedly, without thinking how peculiar my action might seem, I stopped the
cab and marched straight up to the front door. The lady there
was most astonished when I asked her if she wanted to let her
house, because, she said, she had decided to do so only the
evening before.

The deal was soon concluded, and for many years afterwards
I lived in my dream house. Later on, still pondering over this
incredible happening, I told this story to Arthur Schnitzler, the
great psychological author and dramatist. He looked at me, and
after a while answered : " Perhaps you didn't actually dream it
until it happened—then you *had* dreamed it." And he proceeded to elaborate an idea of the mind's working that best can
be compared with the photographic process of a cinema film
(though, of course, he could not make that comparison at the
time, since the film was not yet invented). Such a dream as I
had was as if the film had been run backwards. . . . At this
time Schnitzler had written his play *Paracelsus*, which, nowadays,
we would call psycho-analytical, because in masterly words it
describes the depths of the soul beneath the soul.

As so often happens in the course of history, the dreams of
poets and philosophers have paved the way for the work of the
scientists. At the time when Schnitzler wrote *Paracelsus* and it
was being admired but not understood, I went one day to the
laboratory to fetch my husband, and saw there, sitting on a high
stool in front of a microscope, a man whose pale, thoughtful face
I felt to be interesting and sympathetic. Who is he? I asked
my husband, and when I was told " Doctor Sigmund Freud ",
I was impressed, for I realized what this name would mean to
future generations. . . .

It did not take long for our house to become the centre of a
circle of friends, a mixture of the artistic, scientific and academic
worlds. I, who had been used from my earliest youth to acting

as hostess—true, rather an unconventional one perhaps—to the widely diversified groups of Viennese society that assembled at my father's house, found considerable pleasure being a hostess in my own right at our " dream house ". Here we soon discovered another attraction, not one that I had dreamed of—the big walnut trees in the garden were the very same trees under which Beethoven had sat (there were no houses built around us at that time) and written some of his music. One of our regular visitors always used to tease me, saying that it was not to see his hostess that he came, but to sit under the walnut trees and get inspiration. This visitor was Johann Strauss, whose name amongst all the famous names of the nineteenth century is most closely bound up with that of Vienna. At that time he was already an old man, but he still was full of vitality that was expressed in the whole of his body by his rhythmic gestures and the dancing air with which he walked. His thick hair was dyed black, as was his moustache. For nothing in the world would he have permitted a single white hair to have shown.

It became a regular custom at every dinner-party which I attended at his house for me to make a speech. Strauss had once heard me improvise a speech at home, and solemnly declared that from now on I was to be " his personal and private chief after-dinner speechmaker ". And so often, my heart beating with nervousness, I had to make a speech, and then Strauss would run to the piano and end it with some march tune. At the beginning I thought the whole thing was a joke and he would soon forget about it—but Johann Strauss always kept up his jokes. And so, once after a speech that he had seemed to like very much, he knelt down in front of me, saying : " Hail to the most marvellous and witty woman in Vienna. From now on I will always greet her on my knees." And so he did ! Where and whenever we met—in our homes, at an official reception or at the Opera House —Strauss always greeted me on his knees. . . .

Johann Strauss used to say, " I never know when I am going to miss my best tune," and he was always terrified that one day the perfect melody would come into his head and he would forget it before he had time to write it down. At night he always kept a pencil on the table beside his bed, and often he would write musical phrases and scraps of melody on his pillow-case or sheet.

One evening when Alfred Gruenfeld, the great pianist, was at his house, Strauss turned to him and said: " Listen, to-day I have written a really good tune. Please, will you play it for me."

" Certainly," said Gruenfeld. " Where is it? "

" Just a moment, I must copy it out from my bed." And off he went to the bedroom. A few moments later he came back, very downcast. The sheet had gone to the laundry, his tune had been washed away, and it had gone right out of his head.

As I have already mentioned, Professor Kraft-Ebbing had come to Vienna from Graz at the same time as we had. From the very beginning he had followed with great interest Professor Charcot's researches on hypnosis. Later he himself carried out many such experiments. One day our friend Girardi came and told us that a remarkable medium had arrived in Vienna, who when put into trance would say the most amazing things. We decided to have a séance at our house, under the direction of Kraft-Ebbing. We sent out about sixty invitations, many of them to the members of the medical faculty, including, of course, Bilroth.

The medium, a very pale, very young woman, was put into trance by Kraft-Ebbing. Most interesting things occurred, which need not be described now. To-day they are well known; thirty-five years ago they were astonishing. There is one scene though that I would like to mention, because I shall never forget the shock that it gave me.

Kraft-Ebbing whispered something into the medium's ear; she grew agitated and nervous, and shortly afterwards woke from her trance. She walked shyly around the room, and without any of us noticing it, she removed a watch from Girardi's pocket with the dexterity of a professional pickpocket, and then handed it to Kraft-Ebbing.

At this moment Bilroth, who had already been making

obvious signs of disapproval, jumped up and shouted angrily :
" Enough of these nasty tricks, this is a farce, an absolute
scandal! " And he turned to Kraft-Ebbing, who was standing
in the middle of the room, and added : " You are a swindler! "

Such a scene amongst the most distinguished university circles
was appalling. My feelings as a hostess can be imagined; I
longed to sink through the floor. However, by making a great
effort I succeeded in smiling as if the outburst were nothing but
a joke, took Bilroth's hand, and led him into another room. . . .

At this time there were two current problems of extreme social
importance. I was closely involved in both of them, through my
father and my husband. One was the question of the admission
of female students to the universities. Emil Zuckerkandl was
strongly in favour of it; and, as a matter of fact, I believe that he
was one of the very first people in Europe to take up this cause
successfully. I remember that the Dean of the University argued
that my husband, as an anatomist, should know perfectly well
that women's brains were less developed than those of men. My
husband answered that he also knew perfectly well that " out of
a hundred male students who tried to pass their medical examina-
tions ninety-seven were complete asses, and it could reasonably
be expected that not more than ninety-seven out of a hundred
women students would be absolute geese."

And when his endeavours were crowned with success and
women were admitted to the medical faculty, he was the first to
choose a woman for his assistant—Frau Dr. Bien, who subsequently became one of the most famous of children's doctors.
Trouble arose from this at the very first lecture, when Dr. Bien
had, as was usual for an assistant during an anatomical lecture,
to take round prepared specimens of the organs that were being
discussed. The organs in question were those which were not
usually mentioned in a gathering of both sexes. The students
began to shout and whistle and protest. Zuckerkandl sent for
the porters to throw them out of the lecture room. It was the first
and last protest that they made.

The other problem at this time with which I was connected was that of popular education for the masses; this was a social rather than a socialist movement, and it became of extreme importance at the beginning of the twentieth century.

A number of people, convinced fighters for the idea that it was essential to raise the intellectual level of the people by means of popular science, who believed in this from a sense of justice and also from the conviction that such an intellectual democratization was necessary to prevent the spread of revolutionary ideas, united to found the "Wiener Volksheim" (Vienna people's house).

This establishment was meant for all types of working people. This project, which corresponded with many ideas held by my husband and myself, I supported actively. Until the fall of Austria on March 11th, 1938, the "Volksheim" with its library, its lectures and discussions, its educational courses, was the centre of the ambitions and spiritual energies of a highly gifted nation. The peak of its achievement was reached in the first decade of the century. My father, whose intelligence had immediately grasped the full potentialities of such a movement, decided to support it with his great journalistic gifts and enterprise. In the year 1900 he founded the periodical *Wissen fuer Alle*—"Knowledge for all"—which appeared every week, and was a paper on entirely new lines, devoted to the service of social ideas, which would give the ordinary working man whose leisure time was limited the opportunity of exploring fields of contemporary knowledge that were then expanding so brilliantly.

For a long time my father thought this idea over, and discussed it repeatedly with the great chemist and statesman Marcellin Berthelot.

Marcellin Berthelot had been among the first to deny that the formation of organic substances required the intervention of some vital activity—a belief generally accepted at that time. His investigations of explosives had enabled him to render important services to his country as President of the Science Committee during the siege of Paris in 1870-71. Later he had been Minister of Public Instruction—and problems of education, wherever he encountered them, were dear to his heart.

Berthelot ardently advised my father to start the new paper, and they had a long correspondence about it; unfortunately only one letter from this correspondence has been preserved.

This is Berthelot's letter :

MY DEAR FRIEND,

The message that you intend to found a periodical based on the idea of promoting popular scientific knowledge gives me real pleasure. You know about my endeavours to initiate a similar movement in France. I am chairman of the " Association Philotechnique ", which had eleven thousand members of both sexes. My belief is deepening that a love of science leads the human spirit to a real valuation of absolute truth. Science is an unequalled school for moral frankness and modesty. . . . Also it will lead to the final disappearance of the demand for privilege and the egotistic wishes that separate individuals and nations, so that solidarity will not remain an empty word. Solidarity is not a mere abstract idea, but part of the whole nature of modern science, showing the way for its development.

The antagonism of nations and individuals has always led to wars and imperialism, and always ended in ruin. For every hurt committed against a nation or an individual is a loss to all—a loss to the community.

That is why it is good to bring the works of science close to all people. Because its work is for peace! I fear that this view will not become general quickly enough to prevent the serious international conflicts that threaten modern nations. But just because of this we must foster scientific education by all the means in our power, that it may succeed in postponing this danger, these struggles, these disasters!

You intend to call your periodical " Knowledge for all ". May it help to a " peace for all "!

Yours,

MARCELLIN BERTHELOT.

135

Fourteen years after he had written these words, praising science as a guardian of peace, chemistry was to furnish the most dreadful weapons of destruction in the world war. Berthelot, the greatest chemist of his time, did not foresee that it was his work for science that was to help forge the means by which his work for peace was to be destroyed.

CHAPTER II

WHENEVER Georges Clémenceau came to Vienna, even if it were only for a short time, there were certain items of his programme that were always the same. " This morning," he used to say to me, " we will go and pay a call on two of our old friends." I knew just what he meant and where he wanted to go, so without anything further being said I told our coachman, " to the Liechtenstein Gallery ". For that was always our first call. When we arrived there Clémenceau, despite his age, ran up the steps like a boy and hurried through the rooms without stopping until we came to Rembrandt's " Man with the Feather ".

In front of this we stayed for a long time. " Look at it," he said. " No other master has ever accomplished just this, has ever caught and reproduced this real sunshine, this hot, dancing sunlight falling upon the face of a man. Every time I see it I am astounded and can't understand how he has done it."

From there we went to the Museum of the History of Art. Here, too, he went straight to the Rembrandts, to the portraits of his son Titus, which Clémenceau described as " the tragic youth who searches for death with his soul ".

Then we had a pious little session in front of Breughel— " the great Dutchman who revived the primitivism of the Greeks ". And lastly, a caressing look at Correggio's " Leda ", of which Clémenceau said—" All the charm and grace of the eighteenth century has its roots in this work. Without Correggio—no Watteau."

I spent the summer of 1900, the year of the Paris Exhibition,

137

in the Vendée, at l'Aubrey, my brother-in-law Paul Clémenceau's estate.

One day Georges Clémenceau said to me, " You must come with me to see the Centenary Exhibition of French painting. It is miraculous. Never again shall one be able to see such a concentration of masterpieces.

" Hitherto unknown masters are resurrected here. They have been brought from obscurity to be honoured as precursors of painters whose works have been collected together for the first time in the two big halls of exhibition. Those who once for a short time filled the salons with crowds eager to have a look at the forbidden, the unspeakable, are the great ones, placed at the peak of a hundred years of artistic development."

Clémenceau had been Edouard Manet's friend ever since their early youth. Together they had lived through the times of the struggle of the impressionist—that body of painters who had to fight more battles than their confrères of any previous artistic movement. Georges Clémenceau's passionate love for all creative expression of the human spirit had made it easier for him than for the majority of his contemporaries to cross the bridge connecting the great art of the past with that of the present.

After my experiences in Vienna I was more than delighted to go to the " Centenaire " with Clémenceau. The note about it in my diary begins: " June 17th, Paris World Exhibition. Déjeuner at Georges. Then a visit with him to the Centenaire. . . ."

Passing through the galleries of this apotheosis of French Art Clémenceau was happy and deeply moved. " To begin with," he said, " I want to show you all those masters who now, for the first time, have been hung in their rightful places, those who have been forgotten or misjudged and who now have been recognized as the most important links in the chain which has led to the present development. Look at David, who has up to now only been valued as a classicist and historical painter —look, here he is shining out as a wonderfully vivid portraitist."

(Twenty-five years later the Louvre rearranged the David room in accordance with this idea.) " Can you understand how a master like Chasserieau has not been discovered before? Look at this—the ' Two Sisters ' and this—' Esther '. If you know how to look you will see in them the union of two opposites —Ingres and Delacroix. In Chasserieau you can trace the influence of both these masters whom, up to now, we have regarded as the exact opposite one of the other, and yet who *both* are the ancestors of impressionism."

We entered the Corot room. Between the dreaming summer evenings of his landscapes hung portraits of women, quiet, apparently unmoved. But they blossomed with the same heavenly softness and serenity that suffuses the landscapes; they were alive with the same magnificent and secret atmosphere that floats around his birches. " Truth finally emerges," said Clémenceau. " Remember that Corot's landscapes, which made him famous, represent only a minor part of his genius. In my opinion his real greatness is reached in his paintings of women. And the poor devil could only get his models in secret. When, instead of painting his highly-paid landscapes, Corot followed his inspiration and created a woman upon the canvas, his wife and his friends foamed with rage and spat out abuse, and dreadful scenes took place. So that shy, peaceable Corot began himself to have doubts about his portrait painting. But all the same, he will owe his immortality less to his landscapes than to those serene women who seem so alive here."

Clémenceau introduced me to Daumier and made me realize that he was a newly-discovered phenomenon as a painter. Then he took me to the Barbisonists, to Delacroix, to Ingres, to Courbet.

" This conquest of light—the ultimate achievement of the impressionists," said Clémenceau, " can be traced from two sources. Many years ago, when Monet went with Pissarro to London, he encountered Turner's pictures for the first time. Perhaps Monet felt unconsciously that those foggy canvases that trembled with a single sunbeam could be deduced from

Claude Lorraine. It is a magnificent example of the continuity of a nation's art, that a master like Claude Lorraine who has been accounted a classicist, should be revealed as an ancestor of the impressionists—those dissolvers of the classic forms."

Then we came to Manet. His early works, in which dwelt a Spanish sombreness, were a background for the shining brilliancy that flooded his later and riper paintings. His formation of planes by colour, his construction of space by the most daring simplifications—it was unforgettable.

"Here Manet shows the second source from which impressionism has risen," said Clémenceau. "The discovery of the Japanese art of the woodcut has given us all a new vision. But for Manet, the abandonment of his first style of painting meant a break with everything that he, as a *bon vivant*, liked. But he did not hesitate; once he had found his artistic truth he gave his whole life to it. The ' Déjeuner sur l'herbe ' found a reception only in the salons of the rejected. The ' Olympia ', though, was exhibited in the Salon in 1865, when precautionary measures had to be taken by the police to prevent it being torn to pieces by an enraged mob."

At the end of our visit Clémenceau said, passionately and thoughtfully, " Can't you see here, as clearly as when you stand before a Breughel, a Rembrandt or an El Greco, that the great and only eternal tradition in art is—Revolution? . . ."

A circle of remarkable people had collected around my sister and her home; and it was there, during one of my visits to Paris, that I met Auguste Rodin for the first time.

Later I spent many hours with him, first in his studio on the Seine, and then at Meudon de Val-Fleury, where he created his " Balzac ". Rodin seemed, in my opinion, not only to be one of the great sculptors of all time, but almost equally great as a philosopher and thinker.

He often spoke to me about the beginnings of his career, his poverty, his almost martyred existence. Because, before Rodin became an internationally recognized genius, he had to

suffer an artist's Calvary in his own country. He had to under-
go the worst ignominy that can possibly befall a sculptor. When
his statue, " L'Age d'Airain ", was first exhibited he was
accused of having made a cast of a living body. People no
longer believed, or had forgotten, the enormous realistic
possibilities of sculpture; they could not believe in the creative
powers of such a great artist. " Forger," screamed the high
priests of the Academy. " Forger," threatened the Law Courts.
" Forger," echoed the mob.

But Rodin carried his burden; he remained upright when
at the unveiling of his monument of the " Bourgeois of Calais "
an unheard-of scandal took place. He patiently bore with the
unbelievable insult that compelled him to execute the statue of
Victor Hugo three times over. He created his masterpiece
" Balzac " and had to see it passed over in favour of a mediocre
bust. And the more impossible it seemed to wound him, to
discourage him, to dam the stream of his genius, the stronger
grew the hatred against him. When, in Paris, a plaster cast
of the " Thinker " was placed for trial in the Pantheon, the
statue was found shattered next morning. Never did a city
struggle so hard to destroy its greatest citizen.

But Rodin accepted his burden, and stood upright under it.
Nothing had meaning for him except the stone under his chisel,
and the solid embodiment of his continual dreams. The
scorners and the haters could not touch him. But he never
forgot them.

On one of the last days of May 1914, the last bright May
of peace, I was sitting with Rodin in his work-room, looking
out into the gardens of the Hotel Biron that were beginning
to darken in the twilight. One of those receptions that mingled
the great men and the great families of France was coming to
an end. This was the sort of day and occasion that the master
hated, because people and talk separated him from his work.
It may have been because of some deep inner anger stirred up
by this, that he opened his heart to me, and began his account.
Slowly and quietly he told me the story of his life, listing every

persecution, every injustice, every meanness, every idiocy, every lie, every ignominy, every crime against his work that had left its scar on the lineaments of his spirit.

Now it was quite dark in the room. His terrible account was closed. He stood up and said, " Never could mankind make good the wrongs they have done to me—not even if I lived for another two hundred years honoured and in peace! "

These words, and the accent in which they were spoken, still linger in my ears; it was the terrible story of his life that made me realize from what sources Rodin drew the demonic strength portrayed in Balzac's despisingly raised head, and the icy power of his " Thinker ". He had shaped his own life and pain in the unyielding stone.

After all these new artistic experiences and impressions which I had collected in Paris, it was natural enough that I could not remain simply an appreciative onlooker of the struggle which was beginning to be fought about the new art in Vienna. I was caught up in that storm of new vision and new sensibility. At first I tried to work for the cause by expressing my feelings in writing.

A group of young artists, who had found my articles to be sympathetic to their own ideas, came to me, and said, " You must help us. Your relations with all that is progressive in France, your love for real art, must force you to be a pioneer and fighter for an idea that is destined to arouse Vienna from its charmed sleep. We know you to be a friend of Carrière and Rodin. Your work can be invaluable for our cause."

And soon we had created the new building of the " Sezession " on the Karlsplatz, and had provided a source of ceaseless laughter for the Viennese, who found its straight lines and its simple beauty exaggeratedly " modern ". But the motto, inscribed over the main entrance, was above all mockery or attack—" To each time its art : to each art its freedom."

Enthusiastically I followed this slogan into action. It was a question of defending a purely Austrian culture, a form of art

Franz Löwy, Paris

HUGO VON HOFFMANNSTHAL   GUSTAV KLIMT

that would weld together all the characteristics of our multitude of constituent peoples into a new and proud unity. For to be Austrian did not mean to be German; Austrian culture was the crystallization of the best of many cultures.

Here too, as was the case in political life during the period 1880-90, the pioneers, that band of striving, idealistic, enthusiastic youth, sought a close contact with the democratic west. It was England, and its pre-Raphaelite movement, that influenced the development of artistic handicraft in Austria, and led to the creation of the singular *Wiener Werkstaette*. Its originator was Josef Hoffman. And, just as one used to speak of the " Morris period " so people have come to-day to speak about the " Hoffman period ". From France spread the new vision of Impressionism and the young Austrian artists looked out upon the world with new eyes. The landscapes of Gustav Klimt, the greatest Austrian painter of this time, are Schubert's songs translated into the language of form and colour. And Klimt's paintings of women remind one of flowers—but flowers that could only grow on Austrian soil, and of the soft beauty woven by the Wienerwald. But because Klimt was speaking in his own language, because he broke away from traditions that had become fettering, he had to live through the same purgatory as did Rodin. But Klimt too was a great man, a great man in himself, not accepting anything beyond the truth of his own soul.

In this fight my weapon was my pen, my battlefield the *Wiener Allgemeine Zeitung*. Although I was a mere beginner the editor gave me absolute freedom and handed me the art critic's columns. Straightway I changed the title from " Art Criticism " to " Art and Culture ". Here I wanted to mirror the whole of the great development that was happening in Vienna at this time.

This was a period unique in the history of art and culture, and I was happy to be in the middle of its storm and strife. Soon I was advised to collect all my " fighting articles " and publish them in book form, as a documentation of these struggles. I called this book *Contemporary Art*. Ludwig Hevessy wrote an introduction, from which I shall quote an extract—not in order to flatter my vanity, but because it gives such an impression of the charged and excited atmosphere of this " Austrian rebellion " in the world of art.

" It was in the salon of the author that the idea of a Vienna Sezession was first discussed. There it was that the small group of moderns who gave expression to this idea first met and began the fight for the revivification of art in Vienna. This spirit of initiative did not desert the author later on. Often it was she who spoke the first words in important discussions; and often it was she who spoke words that no other person could have said.

" Only in our feelings and our forebodings did our goal exist; nevertheless it seemed to us astoundingly definite. There was an inexplicable magic of certainty in our consciousness of being on the right path. We felt the true confidence that accompanies the working out of some law of nature. . . ."

When Rodin came to Vienna in 1902, to visit the wonderful exhibition held by the Sezession and dedicated to sculpture, I took him to see Klimt. Rodin, whose drawings present the absolute essence of solidity and movement, felt that in Klimt he was meeting an equal. And turning to me he said, " These masterly drawings remind me of Baudelaire's saying—' Le dessin de création est le privilège du génie.' "

My husband and I had asked Rodin to a real Viennese " Jause " (afternoon coffee). It was a wonderful June afternoon in the Prater, and all the Sezessionists had assembled there. Klimt was in a brilliant mood and sat next to Rodin, who talked enthusiastically to him about the beauties of Vienna.

I had the coffee served on the terrace. Klimt and Rodin had seated themselves beside two remarkably beautiful young women —Rodin gazing enchantedly at them. Klimt had created an ideal of this type—the " modern " woman, with a boyish slimness and a puzzling charm. The expression " vamp " had not yet enriched our vocabularies, but it was Klimt who first invented or discovered the ideal Garbo or Dietrich long before Hollywood had stamped those figures upon the dreams of young men all over the world. And, that afternoon, slim and lovely vamps came buzzing round Klimt and Rodin, those two fiery lovers. Alfred Gruenfeld sat down at the piano in the big drawing-room, whose double doors were opened wide. Klimt went up to him and asked, " Please play us some Schubert." And Gruenfeld, his cigar in his mouth, played dreamy tunes that floated and hung in the air with the smoke of his cigar.

Rodin leaned over to Klimt and said : " I have never before experienced such an atmosphere—your tragic and magnificent Beethoven fresco; your unforgettable, temple-like exhibition; and now this garden, these women, this music . . . and round it all this gay, child-like happiness. . . . What is the reason for it all? "

And Klimt slowly nodded his beautiful head and answered only one word—" *Austria.*"

CHAPTER III

THE last decade of the nineteenth century will always be known in history as a period of a noble fight for humanity. It was the time of a great moral insurrection. An almost fanatical cry for " Truth " arose from courageous souls—and the whole world listened longingly to their cry.

The " Dreyfus affair ", the martyrdom of an innocent man, unjustly tortured, the crime perpetrated by a Government, the gruesome story of Devil's Island—this touched the conscience of the whole world.

This event, which raised a political intrigue to the heights of Greek tragedy, took place during a decade in which the whole of European culture—its music, poetry, creative and decorative arts—was the scene of a great fight for one aim—Truth. Truth to get rid of cramping tradition, academic lies, artistic corruption! And this longing for truth was to bring a group of noble people to risk their careers, their happiness—everything, to save an innocent man from Devil's Island. So art, culture and politics were for a short time welded together in a fight that was for the honour of all mankind.

At this time Gustav Klimt was painting his " Nuda veritas ", the grand and fearless figure of a naked and chaste woman facing fate. At this time the heroic musical creations of the great composer Gustav Mahler rang out like a fiery tocsin.

In these unforgettable years I lived intensely. I was brought to consciousness of the truth behind the Dreyfus case right at the beginning, when the first whispering rumours of the crime that had been committed against him were being suppressed by those responsible for that crime, and when it appeared that the whole of France, and even the whole of Europe, would believe their denials.

The man who gave me this insight into the truth was an

artist, whose moral greatness elevated him far beyond the limits of his art, a man who used his art to express and communicate to others the deep meanings that he had discovered for himself in life. It was Eugene Carrière—who once said of himself : " I see other men in myself, and in them I find myself again. *Tout est une confidence qui nous répond à nos aveux.*"

During December 1894 Carrière had been painting my portrait. While the sittings were in progress, it was his habit to keep up a conversation with his model, in order, he said, " to catch the reactions of thought and movement ". But now I found that he, who was usually so witty and sarcastic, was changed and depressed. When for the first time I was allowed to look at the half-finished portrait I could not help exclaiming : " Do I really look so sad and thoughtful, as if endless disappointments were my lot? "

" Perhaps it is my own sadness and depression that I have transferred to you," he said. " Your face is pleasing to me because of the slight trace of melancholy that we have in common. And now I am deeply depressed because I know of a crime that is being perpetrated, and which I am powerless to prevent."

And then Carrière began to talk about Dreyfus, whose epaulettes had been torn from him that very day during the scene of his condemnation. Carrière became an ardent " Dreyfusard ", and so, of course, did I.

I should like to interrupt here for a moment, and interpose a little scene that took place many years later, showing how the final achievement of such great aims is often wrapped in sadness and melancholy.

When Dreyfus was finally set free, Mme. Menard-Dorient, a violent and courageous " Dreyfusard ", gave a dinner in honour of the occasion. All the leading fighters were present. I was sitting between Carrière and Picquart. Opposite was Zola. But instead of the happy and victorious mood that might have been expected, a heavy, dark atmosphere hung around the dinner-table. Then Carrière leaned over to me and whispered : " *Regardez les, ces désenchantés du sacrifice.*"

Second event—" L'affaire Picquart "—the second part of
" L'affaire Dreyfus ".

In August 1897 Georges Clémenceau came, as always after his
cure at Carlsbad, to visit us in Vienna. This time our first visit
was not as usual to the galleries but to the Central Post Office.
A great heap of letters was waiting him there. Clémenceau
quickly picked out from them half a dozen envelopes, all written
in the same steep, flying handwriting, and immediately began to
read them, obviously forgetting all about the rest of his correspondence, and me as well.

Only on our drive back did he begin to speak—about the
Dreyfus affair, and especially about Colonel Picquart.

Of all the noble figures that had appeared during the fight
for Dreyfus, that test of nobility, his was the greatest. And while
Scheurer-Kestner and Zola were to be thanked for the actual
freeing of Dreyfus, it was Georges Clémenceau who fought
Picquart's battle against the military attack that was directed at
him; and it was he who won this battle and freed him from long
and painful imprisonment.

" You know that Picquart was the *Chef des Renseignments*,"
began Clémenceau, while we were driving up the long hilly road
leading to our house. " He was always very much liked by his
superiors. But this was suddenly changed when, after Dreyfus's
condemnation, Picquart began secretly to investigate the facts of
the case. His researches led him to the discovery that the
Bordereau had not, in fact, been written by Dreyfus, but by
another French officer, a certain Major Esterhazy. This discovery
proved that Boisdeffre, the chief of the French General Staff,
together with all the rest of the staff, had based their attacks on
forged documents. It meant that a revision of the whole case was
now unavoidable. So it seemed advisable to these gentlemen to
get rid of Colonel Picquart, who had become so unpleasant all
of a sudden. He was ordered immediately to Algeria, to join a
regiment stationed there.

" Picquart arrived at Algeria, where his Commandant, Leclerc,
had already received an order to send him with a minimum

escort to the same threatened and dangerous zone in which only a short time ago the Marquis de Mores had been killed.

" Leclerc did not carry out this order because he realized that Picquart would have never come back alive in such circumstances."

Clémenceau stopped for a moment and became quite pale, as he always did when he was really angry. " Then I lost my patience. I said to myself : ' We can get nowhere without Picquart. He is the one man who knows everything. If he has not yet spoken it is because of his military discipline. We have got to get him back from Algeria. And even if Monsieur le President de la Republique Française, M. Faure in person, the whole Cabinet and the whole general staff object to it, I will force the issue—Picquart must return from Algeria."

And by using a remarkably simple method Clémenceau succeeded. For months he wrote in *L'Aurore*—every day in a different and stronger form—" Colonel Picquart, who has been sent to Algeria, is, we understand, able to reveal a number of vital facts about the Dreyfus case. We demand that Colonel Picquart's superior officers should recall him straight away."

They tried not to hear this, they tried to neglect it, but inexorably, every day in the columns of *L'Aurore* was the cry : " Picquart ! Picquart ! " And in the end they had to recall him from Algeria.

In the beginning of January, 1898, I lunched at Georges Clémenceau's house in Paris. He was very excited because Picquart had been put under a military guard after his return from Algeria. I cannot remember ever before or since having seen Clémenceau so pale, so excited, so determined. " What will you do now? " I asked.

" Fight ! " he answered through his teeth, without moving a single muscle of his face.

Picquart was going to be expelled from the army and thrown into prison. At the last moment Clémenceau prevented the case from coming up by exposing the whole enormous intrigue.

Picquart regained his freedom and his rank in the army. The honour of French Law and Justice had been re-established.

Eight years later.

My sister, Sofie Clémenceau, had gathered a little circle of music lovers around her, and, carrying on the tradition of her father's house, she continued to work for a cultured rapprochement between Austria and France—her fatherland and her adopted country. Her friend, General L'Allemand, Picquart, as well as Paul Painlevé, the famous mathematician who later became a leading statesman, were enthusiastic admirers of another friend of hers and of ours—Gustav Mahler. From 1900 to 1908 this little group was present at nearly every concert that Gustav Mahler gave, and often followed him abroad on his tours.

Gustav Mahler! The world is not yet sufficiently aware of the greatness of this giant who strove to conquer the highest peaks of his art. Mahler as a composer is the final achievement of the great Viennese classical school, which began with Haydn and led through Schubert and Bruckner to Mahler.

Gustav Mahler's life programme was what Beethoven expressed in the final part of his Ninth Symphony—*Freude schoener Goetterfunke* (Pleasure, beautiful spark from God). His symphonies are the mirror of the searcher for God in the present. And in their last phase the tortured soul finds reconciliation and peace.

His achievements in the blessed years of his activities at the Vienna Opera House are unforgettable. The renaissance of the opera throughout the world was really the work of Mahler. It was he who created and gave reality to the word *Gosamt-kunstwerk*—the unified work of art—and his influence will last for ever.

When we heard Mozart's and Beethoven's music at Salzburg, admired by the whole world, perfectly rendered, it was to Mahler's influence that we owed the experience. He revived " Figaro ", " Don Juan ", and " Fidelio ", giving them a new

JOHANN STRAUSS   GUSTAV MAHLER

he inscription says : " to the most charming of all
omen, Frau Prof. Zuckerkandl, in friendly memory,
ohann Strauss.")

dramatic life. For he had lived up to his ideal—" to adjust the form and rhythm of space to the measure of music and poetry ". This pure unity was Mahler's work. And if to-day we bow to Toscanini or Bruno Walter, we are also paying homage to the great figure of Gustav Mahler who made their work possible.

His only too short life—he died at fifty—was illuminated by the happiness of his marriage with Alma Schindler, and I am proud to think that it was in our house that he met and straightway fell in love with this beautiful creature, who had loved music and admired Mahler long before my husband asked her to a dinner to meet her idol. It was through her that the hitherto strict and pensive mind of Gustav Mahler found its characteristic happiness of fulfilment. And many of his finest symphonies were written in honour and praise of his beloved Alma.

My sister, who knew and shared in the beautiful friendship that united my husband and Mahler, wrote to me in the autumn of 1906 asking me to deliver the following message to Mahler : That the Paris " Mahlerites " had decided to come to Vienna for a fortnight with the sole purpose of seeing his great achievement—the Vienna Opera House. And for Colonel Picquart, the admirer of Beethoven, this would also be at the same time a pilgrimage to Beethoven's Viennese home.

When I communicated this to Mahler he exclaimed, his face shining with joy : " I'll make a secret Festival for these true lovers of music. A real Vienna Opera House Festival. But no one except us will know about it."

And so he arranged a wonderful and brilliant repertoire. Every performance was a masterpiece, and visitors, the press, and even the court wondered what had made the opera shine with such an extraordinary beauty night after night during those autumn weeks of 1906.

At this time I was just recovering from a very painful inflammation of the knee, and it was rather difficult for me to execute all my hostess's duties. Every day the " French

Invasion " lunched and dined at my house. One rainy day, when my knee was hurting me rather badly, Picquart gallantly took my arm and helped me into the dining-room. He referred to Zola's famous expression during the Dreyfus case—" *La verite est en marche!* "—" Yes," I said, " but unfortunately it is still limping."

Towards the evening of the same day the weather suddenly improved. It became warm, and a real " Indian Summer " seemed to be setting in. We sat in the garden, under the walnut trees where Beethoven used to sit, and Picquart recounted to us how, during all the time he was in prison, tortured and dishonoured, he thought that if ever he was set free again he would achieve two things: Firstly, make a pilgrimage to the places where Beethoven used to work, and secondly, hear Gustav Mahler conduct " Tristan ".

His first wish had already been fulfilled, and the second was about to be gratified this very evening. For to-night Gustav Mahler had chosen for his " secret Festival " to put on " Tristan ".

Picquart was as happy as a child, and as impatient as one; he actually went to the Opera House an hour before the performance was to begin. We had arranged to meet on the main staircase, where he was going to wait in order to help me up the stairs.

Scarcely had Picquart left the house when a telegram arrived. It was addressed to me, and said: " Please tell General Picquart that I have made him Minister for War. He must leave to-night. Clémenceau."

When I had reached the Opera House where Picquart was impatiently waiting I found it hard to tell him the contents of the telegram. So I handed it to him. When he read it he turned pale—but with fury, not pleasure. And losing all his powers of self-discipline and realizing only that he would not be able to be present for the whole of " Tristan " he turned on me, tense with anger—" It was your duty as a friend to keep this from me until the morning—there would have been enough time then. A real friend would not have hurt me so deeply! "

This unjust reproach, together with my regret for his spoiled pleasure, made me angry too, and I turned my back on him and began to limp away. But at this moment the sense of justice, which was so strong in him, awoke and he ran after me, asked me to forgive him; and, reconciled, we went back, and were able to enjoy the first act together. Unhappily and sadly he hurried away as the curtain fell. It was a tragedy for him to have to catch the night train for Paris.

Picquart was Minister of War for five years. This final stroke against the anti-Dreyfus criminals was a world political sensation. But for Picquart it also meant that " the happiest time " of his life, as he called these weeks in Vienna, had been cut short.

CHAPTER IV

GEORGES CLÉMENCEAU became Premier of France in October, 1906. Not only were we personally glad that our dear friend should have attained such a great position, but the event also began to revive in our hearts hopes of a rapprochement between France and Austria. At that time the Balkans were once again the scene of European conflict, as they had been in the days of Crown Prince Rudolf.

By November of 1906 it already seemed as if the main difficulties were near solution and as if our hopes of a real Franco-Austrian friendship were going to be realized—as the following memorandum to the Austrian Government shows. Incidentally, it is a bitter irony of fate that I am unable to name the writer of this document, because to-day, more than thirty years later, the publication of his name might bring him into serious difficulties with the present rulers of our country.

MEMORANDUM TO THE AUSTRIAN GOVERNMENT

I arrived in Paris on Monday, November 19th, and was received on the same morning by M. Clémenceau. I spoke to the Premier . . . of the willingness of our Government to enter into negotiations. This was received with great satisfaction by M. Clémenceau who, on this occasion, repeatedly expressed his desire for an Entente with Austro-Hungary, and assured me of his friendly feelings for Austro-Hungary. He asked me without delay to write in French a detailed account of the situation for the Minister of Foreign Affairs, M. Pichon, so that he would be informed of it in the course of the same morning. I delivered this account at about twelve midday, to M. Clémenceau, who telephoned M. Pichon to say that he had to speak to him about matters of the greatest importance. A talk between M. Clémenceau and M. Pichon followed in the afternoon; and I was asked to call again on Tuesday at 9.30, after the Cabinet Meeting, which the President of the Republic was going to attend.

On Tuesday morning I found M. Pichon with M. Clémenceau. The latter asked me to inform Vienna that the French Ambassador would arrive to take up his post as soon as possible, and that he would have all the necessary written instructions for a discussion of the Serbian question . . . and authority to commence the *pourparlers*. But, M. Pichon thought, and his opinion was shared both by the President of the Republic and by M. Clémenceau, the Serbian discussions should only begin after the Skupstina (Serbian Parliament) had accepted the loan law. They said that the French Government was actuated by the wish to proceed absolutely correctly and loyally in relation to Austria; and they did not want to begin negotiations with mere promises, but only to commence them after they were in possession of a real guarantee of the subsequent execution of their promises. This guarantee could only be the loan, once it had been voted for by the Skupstina, because after that the Serbian Government could not retreat; and France as Serbia's principal creditor . . . will almost certainly have the necessary influence to force Serbia to accept the Franco-Austro-Hungarian co-operation. As a matter of course, this suggestion would have to come from Serbia itself in Vienna. Before the loan was ratified it was not altogether safe to let Serbia know about the plan of Franco-Austro-Hungarian co-operation; as in view of the somewhat unreliable character of M. Pasic, the Serbian Prime Minister, it could not be known what steps he would then undertake.

To make a résumé :

The French Government has given orders to the Marquis de Reverseaux, which are framed in such a way that immediately after the ratification of the Serbian loan law he will go to Baron Aehrenthal, Minister of Foreign Affairs, and declare to him the French Government's willingness to assist Austro-Hungary in

the Serbian question. At the same time, the Marquis de Reverseaux will see that, in Constantinople, the question of an Austro-
Hungarian-French economic co-operation is discussed. . . .

The French Government has proceeded immediately to induce
the armaments firm of Creuzot to give the Austrian ammunition
firm of Skoda some of the Serbian armament orders. During my
stay in Paris the negotiations relative to this came to a successful
end; and the Creuzot representatives gave their binding promise
to transfer the Serbian orders to the Skoda factories the moment
that the French Government wanted them to do so. The French
Government has further undertaken to induce representatives of
the group of French banks that have underwritten the Serbian
loan, to hand over a part of this loan to Austria, if necessary. The
amount handed over would be in accordance with the size of
the orders placed by the Serbian Government with the Skoda
works.

I take the liberty of further communicating an incident that
nearly made this whole undertaking impossible. One day I was
suddenly summoned by the French Premier, who said to me that
he had received news of a nature liable to upset his Government's
strong inclinations in favour of an Entente with Austro-Hungary.
The Austro-Hungarian Ambassador in Madrid had accosted
M. Cambon and said to him that he could see no connection
between the execution of the decisions of the Conference of
Algeciras[1] and the intended Franco-Spanish demonstrations in
Tangier. As M. Clémenceau himself pointed out, this step by
the Austro-Hungarian Ambassador must have been undertaken
on the inducement of his German colleague in Madrid, who had
not wanted to expose himself . . . and he asked me to bring it
to the notice of the Austro-Hungarian Government and make
it clear to them that he, M. Clémenceau, was persuaded that this
step of the Austro-Hungarian Ambassador in Madrid could not
have been inspired by his Government, and must have been taken

[1] As the result of the Conference which met at Algeciras on January 16,
1906, France was able to uphold her claim to a privileged position in
Morocco.

on his own initiative. I took the liberty of sending a note to Vienna on the same day referring to this.

M. Clémenceau had told me about this on Sunday, and when I met M. Pichon by chance on the following Thursday morning he said that he was pleased that at last night's diplomatic reception Count Khevenhüller, the Austro-Hungarian Ambassador at Paris, had made an explanation to him regarding the Franco-Spanish expedition to Tangier that was entirely satisfactory, and had furnished the fullest proof that the Austrian Ambassador at Madrid had not acted on his Government's instructions.

After meeting M. Pichon I went to M. Clémenceau, as M. Pichon had asked me to be the first to give him the good news about Count Khevenhüller's declaration.

I saw M. Clémenceau again last Wednesday, and he said that in view of the Serbian Skupstina's obstruction of the ratification of the loan, it had to be taken into account that the loan law might not be passed, and the Pasic Government would fall. He added that I should let it be known in Vienna that the French Government was in such a case ready to come to an understanding with the Austro-Hungarian Government, about joint procedure in the Serbian question. Such an understanding would, of course, always be based on the transference of part of the Serbian armament orders to the Skoda works. He asked me to find out what would be the wishes of the Austro-Hungarian Government as to the form of any joint procedure with France that might have to be undertaken with the new Serbian Government, and requested me to let him have a note on it at the earliest possible moment.

So I left Paris on the same day and take the liberty of submitting herewith this report for your Excellency's consideration.

My almost daily meetings with the French Premier made it possible for me to get an insight into many questions that are not of purely French interest and concern. First of all I should like to make a few observations about the Anglo-French relations. As is known, the French Premier's declaration in the

Senate about an Anglo-French military convention had given rise to great excitement, especially as the declaration was made in rather a mysterious and puzzling way. I was with M. Clémenceau on the day after his speech in the Senate, and we discussed the fact that his declaration had given rise to some disquietude in the Berlin Press. M. Clémenceau said to me: "I cannot understand this, because it really would be rather difficult for anyone to tell even me what I actually did say. It was my intention to say a great deal, without saying anything."

After a number of hints, given with obvious intention, I have every reason to believe that, in a technical sense, no military convention between France and England exists; but that there do exist very far-reaching agreements to the effect that, if certain situations arise, France and England will help each other with all their power and by every possible means. As far as I could make out, these situations are mainly concerned with the defence against any attack that might be launched against the territorial integrity of either of the two countries, or against any attacks that would endanger the execution of the Anglo-French Agreement.

With regard to the struggle between the Church and the State in France, M. Clémenceau assured me, on my last day in Paris, that it will never be possible for the Pope to force the French Government to create martyrs. He will not close a single church, imprison a single priest, or disturb a single Mass. Oddly enough, said M. Clémenceau, it was Briand, the Minister of Public Instruction (who had always acted in a conciliatory way up to now), who had behaved and spoken very fiercely at the last Cabinet meeting, and had demanded the closing of several churches. He himself had declared that as long as he was Premier he would insist on preventing any forcible measure that could interfere with the freedom of religious observance. Whereupon M. Briand recanted. M. Clémenceau believes that it will not lead to any serious conflict, especially as a considerable part of the French Episcopate followed the orders of the Pope with the greatest reluctance, and would at all times be ready to conclude a peace with the Government. . . .

(The following notes, which were in the same handwriting, were added to the manuscript of the above memorandum in September 1914, when the writer obviously must have been going through his old papers, editing them and putting them into order.)

At this time I believed the success of such a strong bulwark of peace as the Austro-Hungarian-French Entente to be certain, and that nothing stood in its way any longer. Count Aehrenthal and M. Clémenceau, both of whom had then been in power for a short time only, were filled with a desire to show the whole world, by some sudden and courageous act, that from now on a new spirit was reigning in European politics.

But all our hopes were in vain, and our happy expectations bitterly deceived. And it came about in the following way.

The Marquis de Reverseaux had returned to Vienna. Those who were aware of the last week's activities were looking forward to the French Ambassador's visit to Count Aehrenthal. After the first few days of the Marquis's arrival had gone by he called on Count Aehrenthal. *And he did not say a single word about the Serbian question!*

Count Aehrenthal was extremely astonished and excessively displeased. I could not understand what had happened and immediately telegraphed to Clémenceau, asking why the Marquis de Reverseaux had not acted according to his instructions. I received the following answer:

" Paris, December 30th. Because when the representative of the eagle spoke about it to Pierre the latter did not seem to understand. Jacques."

That, in our agreed code language, meant that when the Marquis de Reverseaux spoke in the agreed manner to Count Aehrenthal the latter did not seem to understand.

And with that, in view of the characters of M. Clémenceau and Count Aehrenthal, the mere idea of any Entente between Austro-Hungary and France was lost sight of for the time being.

Each had believed that the other had intentionally misled

him. It was only much later that I found the solution of this disquietening puzzle. The Marquis de Reverseaux was, as he had never hidden, a strict Conservative. He was one of M. Clémenceau's most bitter political adversaries. In him the party man was stronger than the state functionary. From the very beginning he had realized the enormous importance of an effective Entente between Austro-Hungary and France. And he also realized that the success of such a new political combination would be an enormous triumph for M. Clémenceau, and so he did everything in his power to prevent the achievement of this end, and to destroy the work that had already been done.

Several times Count Aehrenthal declared most emphatically that during their interview the Marquis de Reverseaux had not even made the slightest allusion to the semi-official discussions that had taken place in Paris that November, and as a matter of fact he had carefully *avoided* even the slightest reference to the Serbian problem.

The Marquis de Reverseaux simply did not want M. Clémenceau, the hated leader of the Radicals, the Dreyfusard, to have his great triumph; and because of this the realization of the great dream of an Entente between France and Austro-Hungary was never realized.

After some time the truth was perceived in France, and de Reverseaux had to leave his post in Vienna, and did not get another one.

But that availed nothing. It was too late. The great opportunity had passed.

Good heavens, what misery could have been avoided, and how much good done if it had not been for this unhappy incident.

CHAPTER V

THE Clémenceau Cabinet fell on July 20th, 1909. It was defeated over a minor question of the Navy and the Press; and both the Press itself and the Chamber fully realized that Georges Clémenceau could have prevented this fall—if he had wanted to.

Why did he so suddenly become tired of power?

Seldom has there been anyone so difficult to see through, at once so cold and calculating, so impulsive and hot-headed, as Georges Clémenceau. What had made him lose interest in political power for no apparent reason? The death of Colette, his beloved grandchild, a charming little girl of ten, might have contributed to this. . . .

I received the news that Clémenceau would go to Carlsbad this year as usual, then to Vienna, and later to Budapest. I wanted to see him and to distract him a little, if possible. So I wrote to him at Carlsbad, and by return of post received the following reply, which, like all our correspondence at this time, was framed in rather facetious terms:

Carlsbad, August 7th, 1909.

ETONNANTE TOQUÉE,

1. I have never intended to go to Hungary,
2. Nor to Vienna,
3. Nor even to Calcutta.
4. I will leave Carlsbad on the 16th of August for Paris; and then I will go to Mont Doré, where I will look after my lungs.
5. If you come to see me I'll give you a splendid welcome.
6. You may come from Wednesday next onwards.
7. I hope that all the members of the family will give me the pleasure of accompanying you.
8. *Et puis je te salue reverencieusement.*

GEORGES.

Three days later I was sitting opposite him.

I found him aged. His bushy eyebrows jutted out against the world even more threateningly than usual. As always when he was travelling he was surrounded with bags and suitcases filled up with newspapers.

" Now I will become a journalist again," he said laughingly. " Now I am free once more! Now I can laugh and swear at other people's stupidities again, instead of perpetrating stupidities myself."

That was how our conversation started, but it soon turned to more serious matters.

It had been clearly and repeatedly shown that Clémenceau was a friend of Austria. Up to this time he had pursued a policy that was definitely directed towards Austria's good; and his endeavour had always been to lessen and hold back Prussian influence there. Now he was worried about the policy of Aehrenthal, the Foreign Minister, about his annexation of Bosnia and Herzegovina in 1908. And although he admitted that Aehrenthal had always been loyal towards France, he could not but see the great dangers inherent in his Balkan policy. And above everything he was worried about the aggressive attitude of Germany, which now believed itself to be at the peak of her power.

" . . . I am pleased to have got rid of all these responsibilities," he said. " If only for the time being, anyhow. Do you know what I would like best to do now? Write a novel! And, by God, not a novel with an important political background. No! A love story, pure and simple. . . . But one thing is absolutely certain—that after this discussion of ours to-day, I will not be mentioning the word ' Politics ' for the rest of my time at Carlsbad."

On the following day, however, when we returned to the hotel after a long walk in the woods, the porter handed him a telegram, signed by Crozier, the French Ambassador at Vienna. It forwarded an invitation to Clémenceau from King Edward VII to lunch with him at Marienbad the next day.

Clémenceau was not at all too pleased. At first he wanted to decline, find an excuse, say that he was not well. But, bit by bit, he gave in. A friend described in glowing colours how very much he would enjoy the drive there in the beautiful motor-car that he (the friend) would place at his disposal. Then he pointed out how short the interview would be, and so on, and so on . . . until Georges decided to go.

"But you must come too," he said, turning to me.

It was a lovely summer day. At that time a drive in a car was still something new, exciting, and romantic. Clémenceau's friend, who sat in front next to the chauffeur, was passionately addicted to blowing a postillion's horn, and, instead of hooting for people to get out of the way or when we rounded corners, he filled the air with loud and passionate fanfares. Georges, who was in a good mood and had become very frivolous, gave me his hat to wear and in exchange put on mine, which had, following the fashion of the period, a long flowing veil. Astounded stares followed our progress.

We arrived at Marienbad at one o'clock. Clémenceau left me in the hall of the Hotel Weimar, and went off to King Edward's suite. I ate in the hotel dining-room, and afterwards had to wait in the hall for some time, since the interview went on longer than we had expected. Finally the King and Clémenceau appeared on the landing of the staircase. Clémenceau waved apologetically to me, and King Edward bowed with all the charm for which he was so famous.

A few minutes later we started on our way back. Clémenceau did not speak a word, but sat wrapped in thoughtful gloom in the back of the car. I knew his moods well and recognized this one; there was only one thing to do—keep quiet.

After a time he pulled himself together and began to talk, quite quietly, so as not to be overheard by the chauffeur.

"Didn't I tell you the day before yesterday," he said, "that your Austrian policy of annexation might become the spark that would explode the whole political powder barrel? King Edward used to be a good friend of Austria. He always understood the necessity of keeping her apart from her 'ally'—Germany. He has a deep antipathy towards Emperor Wilhelm, and has always been sorry that your Emperor Francis Joseph allowed himself to be so completely led by Prussia in his foreign policy. Now, for years Austria has feared Russia as if it was some evil spirit. For decades this has been the nucleus around which Austrian politics were centred. And now, last year, Austria takes the one sure step that is bound to make Russia her inexorable enemy.

"To-day King Edward spoke to me about Crown Prince Rudolf. He was deeply attached to him. He depicted a Europe that might have been if the two liberal Crown Princes, Rudolf and Friedrich, had reigned together. It would most likely have been a strong Europe, strong in peace and culture.

"Well, after this interview I can definitely say what I always knew. King Edward is an intelligent statesman. It was a bad mistake of Francis Joseph and Aehrenthal to have hidden their plan for the annexation of Bosnia and Herzegovina; and one day that mistake will revenge itself."

"For heaven's sake," I said, "you don't believe in the possibility of a war?"

"To believe in the possibility of a war is to be guilty of beginning a war. No! I believe that in spite of the entirely changed European orientation of power, a real balance might be established that would result in a general quietening down. But to-day one thing has become quite clear to me—in order to rule the East, Austria has lost the West."

A few weeks after our sojourn at Carlsbad I wrote a congratulating letter to Georges Clémenceau on his birthday. He replied on the same day:

Thank you, my friend, but I do not like your idea that a young man of seventy cannot be in love—because I am quite certain, in ten short years, whether I am dead or alive, to be as foolish about you as ever!

GEORGES CLÉMENCEAU

(*from the portrait by Manet*)

My friendship to your husband and to you—*ma vie!*

GEORGES.

September 28th, 1909.

In " ten short years " it was 1919, the date on which Georges Clémenceau broke Austria to pieces.

CHAPTER VI

I DO not want to go into the details of the next few months, months of my husband's illness, months which were filled by his struggles against his increasing weakness and his failing heart. All I need to say is that he suffered silently, without losing his greatness or his good humour. On May 28th, 1910, he died, and the manner of his death was worthy of his whole life.

Only two years later my mother followed my husband to the grave. Thenceforward I devoted my private life to the education of my only son Fritz. But the worries and excitement of the past years began to react on me. I became ill with thyroid trouble. The doctor ordered " no excitement and much happiness " as an important part of my cure.

My greatest happiness during that year was to receive the following memorandum, from the same source as the one previously quoted on the Austro-French Entente. It made me happy because it dispelled the growing fears of war that had been haunting me.

INTERVIEWS AT KIEL

On June 24th, 1912, following an invitation of Herr Ballin, managing director of the Hamburg-America line, I arrived at his yacht *Viktoria Luisa*, which was lying anchored at Kiel. I did not see Herr Ballin on the day of my arrival, as he had gone to inspect the Danish motor-boat *Firnia*. But I spoke to many political personalities, such as Admiral Tirpitz; the Lord Mayor of Hamburg; von Mutius, the German Ambassador to St. Petersburg; and the late Cabinet Ministers Dernberg and von Einem. Most interesting was von Mutius' news that the Tsar wanted to remain on the best possible terms with Germany.

He (the Tsar) regretted that the relations between Russia and Austro-Hungary were not entirely satisfactory, but hoped that Russo-German rapprochement would help to improve those relations.

Herr von Mutius spoke with some satisfaction of the not altogether pleasant state of affairs existing between France and Russia. He is convinced that in the case of any war between France and Germany, Russia would not lend any military support to her ally (France). He thinks that Isvolski's[1] situation in Paris has been somewhat shaken. . . . He spoke very bitterly about Nicholson, the English Under-Secretary of State, with whom he had been in repeated conflict during his period of office in St. Petersburg. Especially did he complain that Nicholson had bribed the paper *Nowoje Wremja* and inspired it with an anti-German policy. Absolute proof of this had been given to him by pure chance, as he happened to overhear a telephone conversation between N. and the editor of the paper.

On the following day I spent three-quarters of an hour with Herr Ballin, on board the *Firnia*, which he had bought the day before for a million and a half marks. He said that the Danish invention of the " ocean car " was one of the most remarkable events that he had known. The end of the steamship had come; from now on it would be possible to go from Hamburg to Shanghai with refuelling. The coaling stations, on which the English hegemony of the seas was partly based, would become useless. . . .

Then Herr Ballin began to talk about politics. The German Emperor, who had often been seen during the Kiel week, was convinced that not for a long time had the international situation been so peaceful as it is now. German-English relations had definitely improved, and it was to be expected that a real trust would grow up between the two nations. It seems that the English idea that Germany is preparing an attack against them is losing ground. Herr Ballin informed me that no one in Germany, with, of course, the exception of

---

[1] Russian Ambassador to Paris.

the "pan-Germanists", had any kind of hostile intentions against England. And he added that the Emperor Wilhelm especially was determined to avoid anything that could lead to warlike complications with England. He believed . . . that Germany would do nothing that could give rise in London to the idea that they were trying to separate England from France. He described the position of the Reichs Chancellor and of the Admiral of the Fleet as very sound. . . .

When, later, Herr Ballin spoke of our Emperor, it was with the utmost admiration. The veneration and almost filial affection of the Emperor Wilhelm for Francis Joseph was really touching. The Emperor Wilhelm was Austro-Hungary's best friend, and the Hapsburg Monarchy could rely on him absolutely. Recently the German Emperor had repeatedly expressed his opinion that the German policy in the Balkans had to be conducted first and foremost according to Austria's interests.

As far as the economic situation was concerned Herr Ballin believed it to be extraordinarily good. He thought that the present upward trend would further improve. At the end of our discussion Herr Ballin spoke at length upon the tendencies that were apparent in Austria relative to the problems of imigration. . . .

INTERVIEWS IN LONDON

Wednesday, July 5th.

I was received at twelve midday by Sir Arthur Nicholson, the English Under-Secretary for Foreign Affairs, to whom I had been introduced by the English Ambassador to the Court of Vienna.

Our interview lasted until after 12.30 and was concerned with current questions of international politics. Nicholson spoke of England's adherence to the Entente with France and Russia as being the basis of English foreign policy. England would be ready to enter into a new friendship with great pleasure, but not at the price of sacrificing her old attachments. The mistake of German policy had been her attempts to separate

England from France. That was the cause of the great tension between Germany and England last year. However, it now seems that Germany has abandoned this idea. The new Ambassador in London, Freiherr von Marschall, has made an excellent impression. One could draw the conclusion from this diplomat's remarks that Germany's policy did not pursue the aim of disturbing the Franco-English Entente. Excellent relations between Germany and England could be established.

After this Sir Arthur Nicholson spoke appreciatively of Austro-Hungary's loyal and consistent policy. He agreed that England's behaviour during the annexation crisis had not always been above reproach, and that the English Government had committed many mistakes, owing to misleading information. But as a result, especially, of Cartwright's[1] reports, the Government had modified its earlier point of view, and had the liveliest wish to keep on friendly relations with Austro-Hungary. Vienna could be absolutely certain that mistakes such as those committed during the annexation crisis would never take place again.

Nicholson spoke about Italy, and blamed her for quite unnecessarily beginning a war,[2] whose end could not be foreseen, and which could provoke all kinds of complications. He saw no possibility of peace being brought about by diplomatic action. Mediation was hopeless, and a conference dangerous. England would remain absolutely aloof, whoever might suggest a conference. (This was obviously an allusion to France.) The whole Mediterranean problem is closely connected with this war, and is creating great concern in England. The idea of an Anglo-French Alliance in which the protection of the Mediterranean would be left to France is unthinkable, for the reason that the French Navy is just as inefficient as the French Army is efficient. England had no other choice but to strengthen its

[1] British Ambassador in Vienna.
[2] Italy gave the Porte an ultimatum of twenty-four hours on September 28th, 1911, and occupied Tripoli, Cyrenaica and the Dodecanes islands, and then bombarded Prevaza without any provocation.

naval power in the Mediterranean, without weakening its northern naval strength, so that it would be prepared for all eventualities.

Among the eventualities Nicholson includes, in the first place, the question of the Aegean Islands. He thinks that, after a peace had been concluded, it would be impossible to re-establish the *status quo ante* on the islands which had been occupied by the Italians. This could not remain without provoking serious reactions in the Balkans, the more so since the situation in Turkey was dangerous, and in any event of a civil war there the Balkan states could scarcely be held back from an attack. The whole eastern question could easily flare up, and it was really fortunate that, following Aehrenthal's proposition, all powers were in constant contact and able to decide on a common policy at any given moment. Whether Italy would occupy still more islands or whether it would try to force the Dardanelles was still uncertain. At the present moment such actions were not to be expected, but Italy had refused to accept any sort of obligation, and had kept an absolutely free hand in regard to the Aegean and Dardanelles. So it was possible that, under pressure of public opinion, the Italian Government might undertake dangerous actions in the late autumn or winter.

Nicholson regards the situation in China very pessimistically. He foresees the downfall of the Republican régime, and fears that anarchism will take its place. In these circumstances he believes that it is impossible for the Chinese Loan to be granted.

As far as Persia is concerned Nicholson thinks that they can carry on there in the same way as they have been doing. The most important factor was that, following the Anglo-Russian understanding, no dangers of international complications were inherent in the Persian question. The establishment of a condition of order in that country was a task that would take a long time.

At the end of our interview Nicholson spoke of Cartwright

with the warmest praise, and described his position as very stable.

From Sir Arthur Nicholson I went to Mr. Tyrell, Sir Edward Grey's secretary, with whom I had an interview for over an hour.

At the very beginning of our talk Tyrell told me that there was a definite improvement in Anglo-German relations. Freiherr von Marschall had made a really excellent impression. He had declared that he had come without any bias, especially without any bias from the German Press, in order to form his own independent judgment. As far as it has been possible for him to form an opinion during the course of his short stay in London, he came to the conclusion that many misunderstandings about England were prevalent in Germany. In particular he was unable to find a single anti-German, despite the talk, in Germany, of there being so many.

This friendly speech of the Freiherr von Marschall had produced an excellent effect, and Tyrell believes that a period of friendly relations between Germany and England is about to begin. Absolute confidence between the two countries really depends upon the " Flottenfrage "—i.e. whether Germany would further expand its naval power in such a way that England would be compelled to see in it a threat to her own safety.

Tyrell spoke about Italy with the same condemnation as did Nicholson. . . . Arising from this Tyrell spoke of the Mediterranean question, saying much the same as had Nicholson. Incidentally, he violently blamed the Italian Embassies in London and Paris, who were pressing for energetic Italian naval action in the Aegean, and acting as propagandists for this.

Tyrell spoke with great appreciation of the intelligent, moderate and decisive policy of Count Berchtold, who has proved to be such a worthy successor of Count Aehrenthal, and who fully understands the value of an independent Austro-Hungarian foreign policy.

At the end of our conversation Tyrell praised Cartwright's activity in Vienna really enthusiastically, and said he had the absolute confidence of the King and the Government.

I should like to add that from both these gentlemen's remarks I believe that I can confidently state that Lloyd George's position in the Cabinet is no longer as strong as it used to be, and Churchill is apparently in the leading position there now.

THE SITUATION IN FRANCE

From London I went to Paris. There, the whole of public opinion is centring upon home affairs. Everyone to whom I spoke expressed the opinion that the question of the Republic itself was the order of the day. But while some hold the opinion that the law of Proportional Representation would save the Republic, others believe that such a reform would lead the Republic into an abyss. But they are all agreed in their firm conviction that the present state of affairs cannot continue. As at the time of Boulanger, an anti-parliamentarian movement is growing. And even the oldest Republicans have to confess that the Republican system has lost much of its credit and is in danger.

I shall relate as briefly as possible the contents of my interview with M. Clémenceau.

M. Clémenceau, who has assumed the leadership of the movement against proportional representation, admits that the Bonapartists are developing an agitation that is not without success. But he believes that it could only become a real danger to the Republic in the case of Proportional Representation. This electoral reform is absolutely opposed to the whole spirit of French history. . . . In the case of the passing of this law . . . the monarchists and the socialists would become so strengthened in Parliament that only a very weak Republican majority would remain. A Government without power or respect would exist, and very soon France would have to face the decisive question— either a monarchy, or a revolution. At such a moment the danger of Bonapartism would arise. In fact, Proportional Representation would lead to Civil War. And that is why he decided to fight against it with all his power; he said that he was convinced that the law, already passed by the Chamber, would be turned down by the Senate.

The majority of the Ministers in the present Government were against Proportional Representation. Jean Dupuy, Minister of Commerce, had told him that twelve members of the Cabinet were against it. But when he (Clémenceau) told that to M. Briand, the latter said that Dupuy was exaggerating, and that there were only ten who were against it. M. Clémenceau believes that the driving force in the Cabinet was M. Millerand, who had excellent connections with the Right. All French political circles are now so concerned with electoral reforms, which have become a question for the whole Republic, that all attention has been withdrawn from foreign affairs. The fight against proportional representation will reach its most acute stage in the autumn.

The same opinion of the Italo-Turkish war is prevalent in Paris as in London. About Turkey they feel as pessimistic on the Seine as on the Thames. . . . Turkey is believed to be hopelessly lost.

Poincaré's foreign policy is very sharply criticized. He is reproached for the deterioration of the relations with Italy and Russia, of neglecting the good relations that had been maintained in the past with Austro-Hungary, and the lack of improved understanding with Germany. In London also people were not pleased with Poincaré. Especially because he had not been able to bring the Franco-Spanish negotiations to a successful end. Poincaré's journey to St. Petersburg is looked upon with serious concern, as he intends to ask the Tsar for the dismissal of Isvolski, and it is feared that the Tsar will not agree to the demand. . . .

———————

After two years I made a temporary recovery that permitted me to go to Paris and see my sister.

It was May 1914—a wonderful spring. Was it that everything seemed rosier to me because my long illness had ceased, or was it that people really felt that this was the last summer of the old, peaceful Europe, and wanted to enjoy it? The fact remains that Paris seemed bubbling over with life and gaiety.

I spoke only to one man who was gloomy, and full of fear and apprehension. It was Georges Clémenceau.

We dined *tête-à-tête* in the Rue Franklin. He shouted at me, as if I had been personally responsible for the follies of Austrian politics : " Have you all gone mad? What is this criminal policy that Austria is carrying out? I am only too well informed and I realize too well where all this is leading to. Austria will start a world war! Tell that to these —— on the Ballhausplatz. It won't help, but at least it might be said."

What had so excited and upset Clémenceau on this lovely evening? I shall never know. I did not want to believe him, I could not believe him. Only the following morning Mercereau called on me as a representative of a group of young people who had united to make peace everlasting, and who had written a beautiful manifesto for world love. He handed it to me with the words, " It is time for us, the people under thirty, to take the reins of policy now. We don't want to hear anything about revenge, anything about hatreds and bloody memories. We are stretching out our hands to our contemporaries across every frontier. No longer shall a handful of old men decide the fate of the millions of the youth. We are going ourselves to build up a new, strong, and peaceful Europe."

I took the manifesto with me to Vienna, to get it published at a time when it would be most effective. . . .

How could I know then how soon this time would come and what it would bring forth? . . .

PART III

CHAPTER I

FOR my sister Sofie France had become a second fatherland. It was a country that appealed to her soul and her character. She had a brain unusually disciplined for a woman, and her thought was exceptionally logical. And there was nothing she cared for more than freedom and progress. From our father she had inherited an excellent understanding of politics.

It was her destiny to become French; she loved her second fatherland passionately.

When the war broke out my sister and I had to bear the dreadful pain of an apparently complete separation. But we never became lost to each other. Never! Her soul belonged to France—and in my blood was Austria! But both of us had a third fatherland, where there was no war, no hatred, no fratricide. It was not of this world. Only those who never lose their love and faith in humanity can become citizens of this land.

Perhaps it was mere chance, or perhaps it was the inner necessity of both our lives that brought about the development in which we shared during the second part of the war. This development is, I think, best shown by the following extracts from my diary.

DIARY

Vienna, October 18th, 1916.

Count Harry Kessler, whom I have not seen since those happy days in Paris, called on me. He, too, believes that something could be done for peace if only a few people had the will and energy to devote themselves entirely to it. We both agreed that as long as we remained here, in this cage, nothing could be done. He suggested that I should go to Switzerland, to the country that in these dreadful days is sought by every friend of peace. We have not decided yet on any definite plan of action. . . .

November 13th, 1916.

. . . I have solved the problem! How right Emil was when he said that every disaster or piece of bad luck inevitably had some good consequences. I can use my illness as an excuse. Only Professor Kocher, in Berne, can carry out my thyroid operation properly. And once in Berne I can try to get into touch with my friends. . . .

Nowadays the idea of a separate peace is taking root in my mind. A separate peace between France and us would mean the end of this most dreadful of all wars. It would be a gain for every nation. Sofie as a Frenchwoman and I as an Austrian could help to bring it about. Of course, I realize that it is my duty not to let our " allies " (Germany) down. And I know that this alliance makes it hard to enter into any negotiations. But the quick bringing about of an ending of the war might also be the saving of Germany. . . .

Vienna, December 14th, 1916.

To-day, in the midst of all this misery, I had a great pleasure, a great surprise. Hugo von Hoffmannsthal called on me. He said that he had always believed that I was a journalist, and he hated journalists. Of course, I have always been much too proud to make the first approaches to this great poet. How pleased I was when he called to-day!

He, too, hates this war. He, too, wants to put all his powers at the disposal of the great cause of peace. Obviously he must have thought that my relations with Georges (Clémenceau), my friendship with him, and the fact that Sofie is his sister-in-law, might be of use to Austria. I was very much impressed by his strong personality, and I think that when we said " good-bye " to each other after our first discussion, we parted as friends already. . . .

I will arrange to make a propaganda tour for Austrian art on behalf of the *Wiener Werkstaette*. As I have been so closely linked with it, the Government will believe that I have no ulterior reasons for such a tour, and they will probably give it their blessing—also I can point out that while I am away I can arrange for my operation. . . .

Berne, January 25th, 1917.

I left Vienna on the 19th, with many letters of introduction, three of them to the Austrian Embassy here. Jeanne (my maid) came with me. . . .

What a wonderful feeling it was to breathe the air of a country that is free of war and hatred. What a pleasure to get the first Swiss newspapers. I breathed this air of freedom as if I had come out into the open after having been imprisoned for weeks in a stuffy room. One thing has really shocked me though. Until I saw the Swiss newspapers I had not realized with what a dreadful and monstrous tissue of lies we are surrounded in Vienna. I understood immediately that if it goes on like this Austria and Germany are lost . . . and at the same time this has strengthened my intentions and made my will stronger.

This hatred felt by nearly the whole world for Germany, this vast hatred that would be great enough to bring Germany down by itself without the aid of an army, and will inevitably bring about the final defeat—*this must not carry Austria into the abyss too!* We Austrians are humane. We treated the foreigners who were not able to leave Austria in time, with humanity and respect. And, to my great delight, I find that this has been realized and appreciated in Switzerland. Austria must be saved, whatever it costs. . . .

Berne, February 7th, 1917.

With the help of . . . at last I have succeeded in letting Sofie know that I am here. I wrote her to say that my health was very bad and I could not bear the tortures of my illness any longer. . . .

When I went to Professor Kocher's yesterday he said that I

must come back this morning. When I arrived I was told that he had died suddenly. Heaven knows what that means for me —perhaps the saving of my life. I may become healthy again here. . . .

Berne, February 10th, 1917.

Yesterday the telegram from my brother-in-law came at last. It said, "*Ta soeur viendra passer 15 jours chez toi vers mi-février.*" And a letter followed it to-day, just a short one, suggesting the Hotel Beaurivage at Ouchy as our rendezvous. . . .

I gave my letters of introduction to the Embassy. They only know about my propaganda mission. None of them seems to have the faintest realization of my relations with France. But it seems as if the people around me sense that I am in favour of peace, and that I will try to do whatever little lies within my power, to work for its cause. . . . There are many friends of peace here. I met Anette Kolb a few days ago; what a courageous woman she is, as well as a great writer. She suffers dreadfully. Her father is German, her mother was French. Her own heart is rooted in Germany, her spirit in France. It was understandable that we found so much in common. There is Dr. Stefan Zweig here—a great writer, and devoted to our cause with all his heart. . . .

I cannot mention the name of a friend to whom I have often written. It is the person to whom I referred in Part II, Chapters IV and VI. I am including some of my letters to him, sent during my stay in Switzerland, because they show very clearly the form taken by my efforts for peace.

Grand Hotel " Berner Hof ", Berne,
March 29th, 1917.

MY DEAR FRIEND,

The Embassy has just forwarded me your letter and the introduction to Musulin.[1] Thank you very much for it, and I

[1] Austrian Ambassador to Switzerland.

only regret that we had not been able to arrange this method of correspondence earlier. You would have known about the Russian Revolution a fortnight sooner.

Immediately after our first warm greetings Sofie began to speak about the absolute certainty of the Entente's victory, and said, " *Dans quinze jours à trois semaines les Romanoffs auront cessé d'exister.*" Then she outlined the plan that the English had already thought out a long time ago. Lloyd George was its soul, and Georges Clémenceau knew the whole of it. . . . Because of the Tsarina, who had already thrice attempted to conclude a separate peace with Germany, England was in favour of the revolution. But they favoured it also because the Russian people did not want to go on fighting for the Tsar. It never seemed to have occurred to them (the English) that the whole movement might be taken out of their hands by the socialists. However, be that as it may, in England and France they seem to be as pleased about the Russian revolution as we are. . . .

But I had better begin at the beginning. When I arrived at Berne I felt very ill. My throat became very swollen, and I decided to go and see Dr. Kocher straight away. I wrote to Paul, as you know, and asked him to do what *he* thought was the right thing. Thereupon Maria F. received a telegram from Paul : " *Dites à Berthe que oui.*" Then a letter came. A fortnight was allowed, and we were even permitted to stay at the same hotel.

Sofie looked marvellous when she came. So fresh. . . . I shall never be able to describe what she has been to me at this time.

She told me what Paul had said. " You should go to Berta, but without any secrecy about it." . . .

I have heard rumours in Zurich that the Germans believe that there is a growing distrust between France and England. The idiot German diplomats have based a plan on this, to take advantage of it by means of *agents provocateurs*. I could not help laughing. . . .

When I told Sofie about this rumour she said : " That all fits very well with our information, which shows that Germany has made Austria into a vassal state, and wants to keep it as one for ever. With us it is quite different; the agreements for clearing Calais and Havre have been drawn up in such a way that, after the war, not a *single* Englishman will remain on French soil."

. . . Germany had been willing in December to consider a peace that would be negotiated primarily with France, and with England only through France, thus weakening and humiliating England. But the rebuff of the official peace offer made the thing quite impossible for the time being. In Berlin they believe that France has missed her last chance. From now on it will be the English with whom they make peace, and through them only, with the French, instead of the other way round. Because the English have already realized that Lloyd George was wrong in his U-boat calculations. Lloyd George had built up all his food and defence plans on an assumption of the sinking of five hundred thousand tons a month. Lloyd George now knew the figures—which had not even been published in Germany—and they had already reached nine hundred thousand tons a month— and if that goes on for another four months, England will have to capitulate. Not because England could be starved out during the war (that would be absolute nonsense!), but because a hunger epidemic would break out after the war, as they are already beginning to sink American ships as well. Lloyd George was lying to the French, in an even more colossally monumental way than had Asquith. It is believed that Painlevé and Clémenceau will soon be able to verify that Lloyd George has decided to sacrifice France (in a typically tortuous English way) as soon as he begins to negotiate with Germany. The Germans believe that these negotiations will lead to peace by the end of December. Then France will receive nothing, instead of what she might have received earlier. . . .

And now, my dear friend, for something quite different. *I really should not be writing the following lines.* And if I do so it is only for the reason that in a question of such an extreme importance I do not want to be without your advice and help.

But you must swear on the lives of those you hold dearest to keep the following information completely secret until I free you from this obligation. So make not a single allusion anywhere, not even to your most intimate friends!

England (Lloyd George) wants to see a great, strong and powerful Austria after the war is over. England and France nearly came to blows over this, because of the paragraph on Austria in the Entente's answer to the peace proposal. Briand had inserted it without the knowledge of Lloyd George, and behind his back. Now the Parmas, our Empress's brothers, are acting on this, and that is why England had recently sent an Ambassador to the Pope in Rome. His mission is to influence the Pope to prepare, if possible, a separate peace with Austria.

What Lloyd George wants to do in case of the victory of the Entente, is to give Silesia and Bavaria to Austria. If it is not a clear and definite victory, then he will only concede colonies to Germany if Silesia, at least, is given to Austria. But I will get more detailed information later. . . .

There is a plan to send *me* with the aid of the Parmas to the Empress—that is why I must return to Vienna for a month. But, of course, I would only do it if *you* had an audience with the Emperor. I am not strong enough to carry it through alone.

One thing seems certain to me, and that is why I'm going into this so very carefully. For us Austrians—who, in the case of a general peace will be bullied and suppressed by Germany —it means a great strengthening if we play the role of intermediary as desired by England, even if we are absolutely loyal to Germany.

My dear, do not believe that I would ever give my help to an action that would be treacherous towards our allies. But for the sake of *general peace* one should take advantage of this magnificent opportunity. I have just received the first letter, which says that further discussion on the problem will begin next Sunday, at the Countess G.'s. . . . I want to point out to you, and stress it, that there is a connection between the " high-ups " in France and the " high-ups " in Vienna.

So, my dearest friend, I can have your word that you will not say anything about this until I give you your freedom.

Yours,
BERTA.

P.S.—Please keep my letters. I should like to have them back when we meet again.

Grand Hotel " Berner Hof", Berne,
April 2nd, 1917.

. . . only a few lines to-day. Yesterday I again received a letter, saying that the English plan of using Austria as a link has been kept in view. *Georges aussi s'interesse vivement à cette idée.*

Yours,
BERTA.

Berne, April 12th, 1917.

MY DEAR FRIEND,

I returned from Geneva only yesterday. Your telegram has been forwarded to me, and I am expecting your letter.

From my letter of March 29th you certainly must have gathered how much interest there was in a rapprochement with, and a mediation by Austria. I am afraid that since war has been declared by America in the meantime, and since the absolutely undeniable successes of the English on the Western Front, this sentiment may have changed.

It is a heartbreaking thought that if, when I was in Ouchy, I had already been able to get into contact with you without any fear of the censor, many things might have turned out differently. For on the 4th of March I already knew about England's intentions, to which France had agreed. If at this time Musulin had been in Berne I might have been able to have spoken to him. But at that time the Military Attaché, von Einem, was in charge of everything, and he kept a Cerberus watch to prevent anyone making any pacific contacts. He would have sent me away, and so I did not go to him, and the invaluable weeks were wasted.

*   *   *

Now, my dear friend, let me tell you something that perhaps will make you cross, but still, please, listen to it. With the exception of B—— there is *no one* in the German Embassy who is confident. The other day Frau B—— told me: " May God keep my husband's optimism alive up to the end. *We*, who see clearly, cannot share it any longer."

There are great men among the Germans who would welcome a breakdown of the Prussian régime, as it is now, and who regard it as simply a rebirth of Friedrich's Prussia.

Even official Germany does not believe in a final and decisive victory, but only wants a new balance of power. They only want a freedom of the sea. Germany is endeavouring with all its power to establish a future alliance with France. If that is not possible, Germany will try to establish a pact with England, and isolate France. Why then, I ask you, shouldn't we try to find some future allies on our own?

One thing is certain : A weakened Germany, after a peace of compromise, will have more than enough to do to look after its own internal affairs, and will not be of any use to us, as our only ally.

I fear only that the right moment has been missed. Two days after America came into the war I received a telegram advising me to go back to Vienna for a few weeks.

Certainly all Frenchmen are once more going fanatically to believe in their final victory. I wish you could have seen Geneva and Lausanne in the dizziness of the English victory at Arras. And so it will be in Paris.

I wish I could come to Vienna soon, but as I am not certain that I can, please do let me know if you think the way that I am behaving is correct—especially my keeping away from, and avoiding any intimate contact with the Germans here.

Yours,
BERTA.

185

Grand Hotel " Berner Hof ", Berne,
April 13th, 1917.

MY DEAR FRIEND,

As I foretold in my last letter, things have developed in Paris. What a difference there was in the last letter. They had been pressing for a quick decision. And—suddenly we must wait, everything must be postponed. True, the main issue remains—the connection with Austria that is desired and sought after. But for the time being the French regard themselves as victors, and want to clear up everything later on.

By the way, I must tell you that here, and throughout the whole of Switzerland, the feeling that Germany has lost prevails again; but in *all* circumstances—Austria can play a part.

Always yours,

BERTA.

CHAPTER II

AFTER I returned from Switzerland Count Czernin, the Minister of Foreign Affairs, asked me to call on him. Through some channel the Ministry must have learned that I had met the sister-in-law of Georges Clémenceau in Switzerland—and then realized that she and my sister Sofie were one and the same person.

The following is an account of my interview with Count Czernin at the Ballhausplatz.

I ascended the stairs of this historical building, · which seemed to me to be redolent of all the tremendous events that have taken place there. Count Czernin's secretary was waiting for me in a big, bare room whose windows looked out on to the park where the blossoms were in full beauty. A few moments later I went into his office, which was on the left.

Czernin sat at a huge Empire writing-desk (I believe that it was Metternich's). He stood up to greet me. There was only one remarkable feature in his face—his intensely blue eyes. With great courtesy he brought an arm-chair over to his desk, and began—" Dear Frau Hofrat Zuckerkandl. I know your relations with France. And I know the love that you bear that country. I pay all homage to your feelings, as I know you would never permit them to lead you to any unpatriotic action. Please, will you describe to me the impressions that you received in Switzerland."

I replied : " Your Excellency, I will not attempt to hide from you that much of the information that I received was confidential and must remain confidential. Having made this quite clear, I accept your invitation. But if I may, without entering into any details, describe the exact impression that I received in Switzerland, where I had the possibility of getting the fullest information, I can express it in a sentence—Austria and Germany have lost the game."

Czernin looked sharply at me, a questioning, unbelieving look. "You allowed yourself to be very much influenced by the other side. Our information tells us that an absolute defeatism exists in France. It will not be very long before Germany will be able to dictate peace terms."

"Your Excellency, all the fighting forces are tired of the war. When I told my Viennese friends that America was going to come into the war—and this was four weeks before they did so—no one believed me. Well, I was right. And so to-day I ask you to believe me that Lloyd George, as well as Clémenceau, and most likely Painlevé, would be willing to save Austria from the impeding débâcle. The only way out is for a separate peace to be concluded by Austria. But at the same time it can be the saving of Germany also. For if Austria stretches out a hand for peace, much can be procured for our allies."

Czernin answered in a quiet, but very definite manner. "It is not even possible to speak of such a thing. Austria's fate is linked with Germany's. But, if you have the opportunity, you may say to the other side—Austria will be pleased to put herself at their disposal as an intermediary. If peace negotiations can be carried on behind the scenes, it could, for instance, be possible to arrange considerable frontier alterations for France, especially in Lorraine. It could even be suggested that the Brieux Valley should be given back. We would be greatly obliged to you if you could make this suggestion."

That was the end of our conversation.

I had come to realize that the time was not yet ripe for an understanding between the powers of the Entente and Austria. Czernin certainly was correct in regarding the excellent German army as a valuable support for Austria's military strength. But he was lacking in the foresight of a real statesman, and he did not foresee the approaching situation that necessarily and unavoidably would bring us to the final catastrophe.

By the middle of May I had returned to Switzerland again.

––––––––––

DIARY

Berne, May 19th, 1917.

. . . the Foreign Office has instructed the Austrian Ambassador at Berne that I am to be free of control as far as my letters to Vienna are concerned—even the Ambassador was not to open them. And yesterday our first secretary of the legation, Baron de Vaux, handed me a letter personally written by Count Czernin in which he guarantees me absolute freedom of correspondence and movement. The letter was sealed with the great State seal.

Berne, June 3rd, 1917.

. . . by the way, my freedom of movement is not quite so unlimited as in my simplicity I believed at first. The Germans seem to have got wind of my relations with France. They are suspicious, and one of their best political agents has been detailed to follow me. I had not realized that he was shadowing me on my many travels about Switzerland (after all, I *am* here to organize the Austrian art propaganda). I only learned about it yesterday through the Austrian General-Consul at Zürich, Herr von Mauregg. He *is* a nice man. When I called on him yesterday he smilingly pointed to a big dossier lying on his table, and said, " It would be difficult to find another woman with such a spotless private life as yours. Here, among these papers, are all the memoranda written by the agent of the German Embassy who shadows you. They prove that you lead a highly moral life, and do nothing but work." And with the animosity that always has and always will prevail between Germans and Austrians, he added sarcastically : " The Germans had hoped for something quite different."

I don't mind about it. It's quite fun to try and escape this shadower who thinks that he can know every step that I take. Ferdinand Hodler, the painter, who has become a great friend of mine, has promised to help me. His studio has two entrances, and while the poor German agent waits at one of them for me, I shall leave by the other. Hodler is right. More than one German agent is required to keep up with an Austrian woman. . . .

————————

I was, of course, continuing my correspondence with my friend in Vienna. I reproduce some of the letters that I wrote at this time.

Geneva, July 18th, 1917.

MY DEAR FRIEND,

I have again discussed in detail with Sofie the plan to enter into conversations with Austria. She told me that Painlevé had already been talking to Lloyd George for weeks about the Entente's position in regard to Austria. Now they have won Ribot[1] over to their opinion. The one thing that they are now concerned about is how to make Italy sufficiently disinterested to give up its demands upon Austria. Clémenceau stopped writing against Austria months ago. But on the whole he is not taking much part in this discussion.

I have been told that it would be much easier for the Entente powers to enter into negotiations with a Germany that was really strongly democratic. . . .

Yours,

BERTA.

Zürich, August 3rd, 1917.

MY DEAR FRIEND,

Only now have I told Sofie that our Government would be willing to press Germany for possible alterations of the frontier

————————

[1] Succeeded M. Briand, in March 1917, as Premier and Minister of Foreign Affairs.

—especially in Lorraine. I also told her that the Austrian Government and the Emperor Karl did not intend, in case of a victory, to keep Serbia. They would not offer any help for the conquest of foreign territories. Our only demand to Serbia would be that there must be close trade connections between us, and that the Karageorgevic dynasty must no longer rule. As the slogan to the Entente is " No annexations ", this must also apply to Italy, and in no circumstances whatever would we be willing to cede a single foot of Austrian soil to Italy.

In England and France the belief in the separation of Austria from Germany has disappeared. This has been brought about by the declaration that Czernin made to me. In spite of that they are still inclined to negotiate with Austria—about Austria. England has especial confidence and sympathy in the Emperor Karl's democratic tendencies.

The French Government has put forward one absolutely definite demand as a condition for any peace negotiations : the return of Alsace-Lorraine. Georges Clémenceau is in favour of carrying on, without conditions, until May, and by then America's active participation will have become effective. In France they will not even refrain from an active *régime de terreur* against the Pacifists. Another party wants to conform with England, and is still trying to find a way to a quick ending of the war. This party, and Lloyd George, as I have already written, brought Ribot to follow a policy *avec l'orientation vers l'Autriche*. That is the reason why Ribot had instructed the Entente papers to use milder language.

The main obstacle in the way of peace negotiations is the autocratic régime in Prussia. And if no definite change is brought about there soon, then even England has decided to take no steps towards an earlier ending of the war. How deeply a change in Prussia is connected with the general peace situation can be seen by the following remark : " Peace would be possible if there were a truly democratic Prussia, instead of one ruled autocratically by the Hohenzollerns. The return of Alsace-Lorraine is a necessary condition for one special reason, in order to create a glacis against future attacks from the side of Germany, which as long as there is a militarized Prussia will be unavoidable."

However, whatever happens, France is preparing for a new winter of war. By the end of May the Americans have promised half a million front-line troops, and three hundred thousand reserves. And this is only the first of a series. I am afraid that by now everyone must recognize that we and Germany have lost the war.

Berne, September 25th, 1917.

. . . There is not very much to say at the moment, for my main informants are not here.

The news of the state of popular feeling in Berlin is astounding. The mob seems to have become absolutely chauvinist once more. And the whole country, up to the Emperor himself, is *sous la botte de Ludendorff.* They are enraged about the Austrian peace policy and are actually threatening us. Even the Germans in Switzerland seem to share in this feeling. Montlong —who sends you his love—has shown me a letter (without telling me the name of its author) obviously written by a German in a high position, that gives a really faithful rendering of the German credo—" Austria owes everything to us. We had to lift them out of the mud. They had better be careful lest they betray us now. It is obvious that that is what they are considering now. They had better remember that the German Army is undefeatable."

Georges' position in France is powerful. He has become the man of the day since his speech in the Senate that brought down Malvy and Ribot.

Yours,

Berta.

I was in Switzerland right up to the end of September 1918, except for some short intervals. The circle of friends that formed round me increased; I only learned much later that this was partly due to the articles that I had published during the first years of the war, and which had been widely circulated in Switzerland as a proof that there were people in Austria also who believed in peace and were willing to act for it.

But all my efforts seemed to be in vain. My friend in Vienna had only been able to send me uncensored reports about his interviews and impressions since August 1918. I am including one of these reports, as it is significant of the situation within Germany and Austria at this late period of the war.

INTERVIEW WITH THE GERMAN AMBASSADOR TO AUSTRIA

On Friday, September 6th (1918), I called on Count Wedel, the German Ambassador. He spoke of the visit of Herr von Hintze. . . . Hintze had twice spoken to the Emperor, and the interview was mainly on the question of peace. The Emperor Karl most emphatically demands that frank peace proposals should soon be made from the side of the allied powers. Herr von Hintze is also of the opinion that some move should be made for peace. But he believes that the moment is not yet ripe for such an action. He also thinks that any step in the direction of peace must not be made too obvious. The right moment for beginning negotiations would, in his opinion, arrive when the German Army had taken up its new positions, from which they could not be dislodged by the armies of the Entente. According to Ludendorff this would be accomplished by the German Army in the very near future. This does not exactly point towards the " glorious peace " feelings that had existed earlier, and there is no hope whatsoever that any real understanding as to the nature of the step that has to be taken towards peace will be reached in the near future.

Herr von Hintze complained bitterly about Count Hertling, who was too old-fashioned to retain his position of Reichs Chancellor. Count Hertling did not want to come to Vienna because the strain would be too much for him. Herr von Hintze and

Count Wedel believe that Count Hertling will very soon be removed from his position, and they believe that this event will be hastened by the Reichs Chancellor's last pronouncements. The Emperor Wilhelm is understood to be very angry about him, and Herr von Hintze thinks that Count Hertling's successor will be Herr von Fayer, the present Vice-Chancellor.

The Ambassador spoke at some length about the bad feeling that is prevailing in Germany at the moment, and is even spreading amongst the troops—with whom latterly Hindenburg has lost a good deal of prestige. He said that at the front it can often be heard said that Marshal Foch is much superior to both Hindenburg and Ludendorff and that he is altogether a better fighter. The Ambassador again assured me that Ludendorff was absolutely convinced that the Anglo-French offensive will not succeed in breaking the new German positions. The losses of the Entente's armies are surpassing anything that could be imagined in any previous war. But Ludendorff admits that Marshal Foch, whatever he had done before, has done well now. Count Wedel added that for the time being any renewal of the German offensive was out of the question. . . .

While even the highest and best informed circles in Germany and Austria were comparatively optimistic, we in Switzerland already knew definitely that the Entente powers had drawn up their plans for a complete reconstruction of Europe, which would take place after their final victory. To my sister, who had gone back to France, I sent an imploring letter, which, as my correspondence with France was subject to strict censorship, I had written in our agreed code.

Geneva, September 10th, 1918.

MY DEAREST SOFIE,

I am writing this from my chalet, where I am still staying. The reason for this letter is that I would like to know if you still remember the wonderful collection of Boule furniture that we

saw at the antique shop. Couldn't you ask your friends whose
house is to be refurnished by that old collector and his friend, if
they could find a way of using this beautiful Boule in a way that
will not destroy its harmony too much. I have heard with regret
that they are thinking about removing several pieces and thus
breaking up this lovely ensemble. I ask you to tell them that
I, who really do know something about architecture and interior
decoration, most strongly advise them not to. The dismember-
ing of the Boule suite will be followed by the most disastrous
consequences. It would mean that some of the best pieces would
be taken over by people who for a long time have been ambitious
to secure them. You know who these people are, and what an
absolute lack of taste they have. Of course, they will be delighted
if the old collector lets them have part of the Boule suite. And
they believe that they can make a good bargain with him. But
really they get nothing as long as they are getting single pieces,
which, so long as all the parts are together, make up a beautiful
ensemble, but if they are torn apart will never fit properly into
any other house. Please do remember this ardent desire of mine
and see that these antiques are preserved. And please reply
immediately.

Yours,

BERTA.

[*Boule = Austria.*
Pieces of furniture = the countries of the old Austro-Hungarian
    Empire.
The old collector = Georges Clémenceau.
The friend = Paul Painlevé.]

My sister's reply consisted of a telegram : " Wait until the end
of September."

And so there I waited, in the midst of that first dreadful
influenza epidemic, which turned Switzerland, that had been
spared from war and disaster for four years, into a graveyard.

By the beginning of October I still had no news from Sofie,
and so I returned to Vienna.

195

DIARY

October 3rd, 1918.

. . . to my great astonishment Vienna is comparatively quiet, and completely uninformed. The feeling still exists that whatever happens the Austro-Hungarian Empire will remain, like a rock in the middle of a raging sea. At the moment the real centre of interest seems to be the question of who will be the new director of the Burgtheater, and who will be on the new board. That is what this town is concerned about. Anyway, in the end Hermann Bahr has been elected, and I am very glad, because this really internationally-minded man will help us, once peace is concluded (when, when will it be?), towards a spiritual rapprochement with the countries that after four years of war will still be regarded as our enemies.

The play that I was translating in my spare time at Berne, *Les Noces d'Argent*, by Paul Géraldy, a young Frenchman whom I believed to be a real genius,[1] I sent to Hermann Bahr to read as soon as I returned to Vienna. I liked it so much, and I am glad that he read it quickly and immediately accepted it. He means to put it into production quite soon. That is a really Austrian action. It makes me proud to belong to a nation that in the midst of the war will produce a play because it is good, regardless of the fact that it is written by a member of an enemy country.

[1] And who has proved since to be one.

CHAPTER III

THE horror was indescribable. Not only had we lost a war—but the whole Empire had fallen to pieces. Nothing but a crippled torso, unable to move by itself, remained of the Austria that had ruled and united other nations for centuries.

At this moment a new spectre began to haunt Europe—the spectre of Communism. And that little Austria was saved from it was due only and entirely to the Socialists, who had come to power. They manned the barricades against the tide of Bolshevism which was flowing over from Bavaria and Hungary, where Soviets had been set up.

The remains of the Austrian Army, streaming back from the Piave, began to revolt. Demonstrations took place in the streets. Despair spread. . . . Revolution broke out—though it was but a bloodless revolution.

At the Foreign Ministry, which in the interim, after Count Czernin had left, had been taken over by Count Colloredo, complete muddle and disorganization reigned. The downfall of the old régime had begun.

DIARY

November 13th, 1918.

The day before yesterday I was rung up from the Ballhausplatz. They asked me to come there straight away. How everything had been changed in these last few days! The carefully dressed servants, who had known so well how to be at once arrogant and servile, were now very sorry wretches, stripped of all their grandeur. The old Imperial civil servants, whose easy friendliness used to show such a cultured courtesy, crept about looking unhappy. Through doors that were left open everywhere, emptied drawers could be seen, and the roaring fires in the big old-fashioned tile stoves were consuming the papers that had been taken from them. The Socialists were to move in to-morrow, and there were many things that were better burned than left for them.

Count Colloredo and Herr von Wiesner were waiting for me. They only spoke a few words about our desperate situation . . . the threat of starvation and bloody revolution. There was no necessity to *tell* me anything about it, I *know* the danger too well.

"What is it?" I asked. "What can I do to help?"

"To-night the last courier is going to France," said Colloredo. "We implore you to write to Georges Clémenceau. Your cry for help will reach him. Some respect must be shown to a beaten enemy. Clémenceau will believe what you write to him. Describe our situation, describe our misery. And, please, write straight away. Sit down, and write now. The courier is leaving in an hour."

And so, sitting at Metternich's desk, I wrote a letter to Georges Clémenceau. I enclosed the letter in a separate envelope, addressed to Dutasta (French Ambassador in Berne), who had been a friend of Georges for many years. I asked him to forward it.

I prayed to all the Powers that the letter might be read, and accepted in the spirit in which it had been written.

November 22nd, 1918.

. . . Yesterday I was again asked to the Ballhausplatz. This time it was Otto Bauer, the Socialist Foreign Minister, who wanted to speak to me. Although he doesn't realize it, he is continuing the course of action commenced by Count Colloredo and Herr von Wiesner. Once more, how changed the Ballhausplatz was. There were typewriters on the costly inlaid tables, and new faces in all the rooms—carelessly dressed Socialist civil servants.

Otto Bauer had been a prisoner in Siberia. The traces of his long suffering showed in his face, but he greeted me briskly and began straight away:

"World history presented its bill to the Hapsburgs on the 12th of November, 1918. But who has to pay it? The people! And we, the Socialist Government, are left with a situation of poverty, hopelessness, disaster and despair that I believe to be unparalleled in the annals of any defeated country. Austria has suddenly lost its wealth of wheat and coal. New frontiers surround us. There are no possibilities of any imports. So, our next aim must be to secure them from the new enemies who surround us—in peace—now, from the Czechs, the Hungarians, the Poles and the Yugoslavs. Austria is like a lonely island amid stormy seas. How can a disaster be averted?

"I asked you to call on me because I know that you are always willing to help. At the moment the most burning problem is that of food. You might think that this is not my province. But the situation makes it so. The question of provisioning Austria can be solved only by international help and the bringing about of new international relations. These, I am afraid, will largely consist of demands for loans. It is a bitter fact but it must be faced. I know that you have been in Switzerland for two years, working for a rapprochement with France. I know, too, that you have made yourself greatly liked by the Swiss officials. Now, Switzerland is the only way that lies open to us. They themselves cannot give food to starving Austria. But they can be of immense assistance, as a means of communication, as a place through which can come the help of America and, from what is in a human sense more remote—Europe."

"But how can this be initiated?" I asked. "No one on the other side can understand our needs. No one sees our children wasting away for lack of milk, fat, meat, or bread that can be eaten."

"First and foremost: we must forward our demands for organized international assistance to Paris," said Bauer. "Because it is there that the statesmen of the Entente will be sitting in judgment over us. The first thing to be done is to secure the decisive man, the man who has been chosen to help to feed Europe—Hoover. We must forward to him absolutely authentic data of our situation."

"Haven't you done that already?"

"Unfortunately not. For where can we trace this untraceable man? Even in the neutral countries no one knows where he is. His address is kept absolutely secret. This is my plan. Since, during the war, Berne was the focus of all attempts at international rapprochement, and since to-day it is, so to speak, the ante-room to the sanctuary of Versailles, I have decided to nominate an Ambassador to Switzerland, and quite independently send a Commission to Berne. I want to ask if you would be willing to go to Switzerland—but entirely independently, both of the Commission and the Embassy, in order to secure French sympathy for Austria. You, as a woman who won so much sympathy for your peace activities during the war, must be able to arouse the world's conscience about Austria's need for food and coal. . . ."

"I am afraid that you overestimate my influence. I am far too well-informed concerning the world's feelings towards our unhappy country to be optimistic."

"All that we can hope from France is that they will not protest if America offers to help us. Try to gain this point—and try to do it quickly. For if no help comes by the end of December, then help will be too late. Our people will not be able to bear their hunger any longer. A civil war will break out unless help comes soon. . . ."

What woman would have refused to accept this task?

I did not for a moment underestimate the obstacles to be overcome, especially my own personal obstacles, for anyone who knew Clémenceau—who was absolutely all-powerful at this time—would know that the greatest obstacle in the way of anyone who wanted to ask him a favour would be a past intimate acquaintance. He would prefer to be called merciless than biased. My task was not to secure France's help for our country through Clémenceau, but to try and find a way to get France to help us in spite of Clémenceau.

The echoes of the defeated countries' cries for help could be heard at Versailles. Wilson and Lloyd George supported Hoover's suggestion to send a Commission to Berne to deal with the food problem. All the allied powers agreed to nominate representatives to the Commission with the one exception of Georges Clémenceau. It was an unforgettable deed of Hoover to have placed himself at the head of this Commission.

So several men and I, who, by the international connections, would be likely to influence the Hoover Commission, went to Berne. One of them was the famous Slatin Pasha, who had been in the English service as General Inspector of the Sudan up to 1914, and who had returned to the Austrian Army at the beginning of the war, where he had been responsible for the care of prisoners.

DIARY

Berne, November 30th, 1918.

On the dark, misty morning of the 26th we met at the Westbahn in Vienna, where a train, made up of three sleeping carriages, was waiting for us. The station was like a gipsy camp. Not a trace of order—absolute anarchy. Starving refugees mingled with escaping swindlers and pickpockets in the waiting-rooms. It was an ordeal to enter our train in front of this embittered mob, although really by no stretch of the imagination could it be called a " luxury train ". We had been taken on to the platform through a side entrance, but the moment we set foot on to it the news was spread that a number of " bourgeois " were trying to run away to Switzerland in a luxury train.

Everything was ready for our departure, when the mob surrounded the train, pulled the driver from the engine and began to shout, " Get out, you swine, get out. We won't allow you to go. We have to travel on wagon roofs and cattle trucks and you think you can sneak off in a luxury train. Get out of it——" And some of them began to force open the doors.

At this moment Slatin Pasha opened the door of his compartment, raised his hand, and motioned the mob to silence. He began to speak——" We aren't luxury travellers. We aren't rich people going on a pleasure trip. We are going to Switzerland to try and get bread for you. We are going to humiliate ourselves, to beg—for you, to save you from starvation. Let us go. You should be ashamed to threaten people who are going to get food for your children."

The crowd fell back, and the driver started the train. . . .

From this moment Slatin Pasha became our leader. It took two days and a night to reach Berne. The train had to stop for hours at little stations that were like armed camps. When we arrived at Feldkirch, at the frontier, we learned that our train could not proceed until the next morning. So we decided to search for accommodation in the town. Slatin Pasha went out with some other men to look for an hotel. They came back with the news that the state of the inns and hotels were such that it was impossible even to consider staying in any of them. Slatin Pasha, who was travelling with his wife and little daughter, said that in no circumstances whatever should anyone be allowed to spend the night in the town. Again he took command of our little expedition, and asked us not to leave the train until he returned. He went to see the station-master, and after half an hour came back and said: "I have spoken on the telephone with the command at Innsbrück, and I have managed to get permission for our train to be put on to a siding for the night. That means we have to camp in the train. Everyone must arrange themselves as comfortably as possible and I ask your permission to act as forage officer." He was really marvellous, and organized a regular provision service. He had found out that it was possible that the engine might be detached from the carriages, so he brought us some coal and —I will never understand how he managed it—bread, butter, eggs, and meat. He said laughingly, " There was no one who could compete with me when I had to improvise a meal in the desert." And he was a good commander too. When we had eaten he ordered us to shut all windows, switch out the lights and not to leave the train, since we did not know when it would start again.

We left at six in the morning; an hour later we were at Buchs, and we reached Berne in the afternoon. There our party broke up, each trying to find the best way in which he could approach the Food Commission.

(The next weeks were so frantically busy that I only found time to write up my diary after I had returned to Vienna.)

Vienna, January 5th, 1919.

. . . I found that the situation was worse than I had imagined in my most despairing moments. The Swiss Government did not recognize our Ambassador, and that meant that he had no possibility of approaching anyone officially. The fate of the Food Commission seemed to be even worse. It was intended to get the Entente to send an inter-allied Commission to Berne, who, with the help of Hoover, would collect all the necessary information, statistics, and suggestions from our delegates. Three points had been fixed as the basis of any negotiation :

1. Grants of foodstuffs from the Entente.
2. Permission to be given to Switzerland to forward them to Austria.
3. For them to be sent directly to Vienna, without immediate payment.

But everywhere we found sealed doors. For, in confirmation of the rumour that was circulating, Lloyd George, Clémenceau, and Wilson had declared themselves bound by their word of honour not to listen to any proposition that originated from the defeated nations. And orders had specially been given to the Berne Embassy not to accept any emissary or intermediary sent by them. So, I learned on the second day of our stay at Berne, that even the American Ambassador had refused to forward our appeal to Versailles.

The first step forward was the publication of an article in the *Berner Bund* describing the appalling condition of the Austrian civilian population. A member of the Commission succeeded in getting into touch with Mr. N. Wilson, Woodrow Wilson's nephew. Slatin Pasha was able to discover where Hoover really was, and to forward our appeal to him.

It was my duty to storm the French fortress. For they had declared that if Hoover sent a Commission to Berne France would not be represented on it. The absence of France would have defeated the united front that was necessary for the success of such an action. From the beginning I had realized that I would have to secure the help of women. And so I went over the Aare Bridge into the wealthy quarter of the town, where the whole diplomatic corps had pitched their tents. I had a friend there who was of considerable international fame, and a great humanitarian. It was her whom I wanted to approach for help.

She said to me: " I can see only one way out. Some important Swiss personality can at least inform the French Ambassador of your presence here, and the urgency of your mission. I think I can promise to find a way of arranging this."

It was not difficult to convince any woman of the misfortunes, miseries and disasters that the women and children of my fatherland were suffering. I returned to my hotel with a firm promise from her to do everything in her power to help my mission. And when I entered my room I found a bunch of roses on the table, a newspaper cutting entitled " The Press " (which, as a matter of fact, I had written in Vienna a long time ago), and a short letter which said the following: " *Un ami inconnu qui le restera, se permit d'assurer à la femme qui en 1914 a écrit des paroles si courageuses que les portes de l'Ambassade Française ne demeureront pas fermées à son appel."*

I received a message secretly, telling me that the Chargé d'Affaires at the French Embassy (the Ambassador himself was not in Switzerland at the time) was expecting me at three in the afternoon. I used all the caution I had learned from my two years experience of " secret diplomacy " in Switzerland and arrived at the French Embassy seen by no one. I was afraid that the Chargé d'Affaires would receive me in a purely formal way, simply because he had been asked to by some influential person. But I found him to be one of the most warm-hearted and understanding men that I had ever met.

The Viennese Social Democrats were in favour of a union with Germany, but I, of course, was not in agreement with them on this point, and I spoke to the Chargé d'Affaires about a plan that was favoured by many prominent Austrians—to create a federal union of nations, a Danubian Confederation. At the same time I naturally mentioned that the man who had sent me— Otto Bauer—did not believe in such a possibility, because the hatred of the constituent nations would be too great.

At this point the Ambassador interrupted me : " *Eh bien, là il a malheureusement raison. Notre idée était d'arriver à reconstruire l'Autriche. Mais nous avons rencontré une telle haine chez tous que nous ne pourrons y arriver. Mais une union purement économique peut être le vrai moyen."*

My aim was to keep in contact with the French Embassy, and through extreme individual kindness and understanding I succeeded in doing so, and on the 30th of December, my last day in Switzerland, I was able to forward to the French Embassy the following letter and memorandum written by Otto Bauer :

Vienna, December 27th, 1918.

DEAR FRAU HOFRAT ZUCKERKANDL,

First of all I want to thank you most heartily for your endeavours and for your information, which I have read with the greatest interest. I hope that soon it will be possible to make use of the threads that you have started to spin in our interests. Of course, what I should like best of all would be for you yourself to be able to go to Paris.

With regard to the question of German Bohemia, I should like you to communicate the following to M. Clinchant or M. Dutasta, if the latter has returned by now : The Czechoslovak state would, if the Sudeten Germans and the German Bohemians are added to it, possess apart from its six and a half million Czechs, three and a half million Germans, and two million Slovaks, in addition to over a hundred thousand Poles and some Hungarian minorities. The belief of the Entente nations, which has been influenced by the Czechs, is that the Czechs are identical with the Slovaks. This is wrong. The Slovaks have their own literature and language, which is similar to, but by no means identical with, that of the Czechs. Socially and culturally they are fundamentally different from the Czechs. The Czechoslovak state would become a nation in which as a matter of course the Germans, the Slovaks, and the Poles would fight against the small Czech minority. Judging by the last fifty years of Austrian experience, it is impossible to satisfy national minorities with mere autonomy. The least that is needed is a constitution on the Swiss pattern : cantons with legislative power, and absolute equality and freedom of nationality and language in the Government. The Czechs do not even think of doing such a thing. They don't want a Czecho-Slovak-German state, but a Czech national state with five and a half million non-Czechs who at the very most would be given local autonomy. This is certain to bring about an intolerable situation in the course of time.

On the other hand, Austria is put in an impossible situation by the taking away of Bohemia. It means the loss of the industries by means of whose exports the necessary imports of food and coal could be secured. Without German Bohemia Austria has to depend on foreign countries for approximately a third of its wheat, more than half of its animal fodder, and practically the whole of its coal, fat, and sugar. If German Bohemia and its industries are taken away from Austria, with what can we pay for these essential imports?

Nor would a Danubian Federation bring about a solution of this question. If German Bohemia is taken from Austria, the latter would be far the weakest state in such a federation, both economically and from the point of view of population. It would feel as if it was under foreign rule, and revolt against it in just the same way as the Czechs revolted against the existence of the old Austria.

I hope to be able to send you, by the same mail, a memorandum dealing with this question, which might furnish the arguments necessary for dealing with the question of the German Anschluss during your discussions with the French diplomats.

With best wishes, I am yours

OTTO BAUER.

MEMORANDUM

1. *The Food Problem*

The state of food supplies for the population of Vienna is still very serious. There is not enough flour to last beyond January 15th. Although Switzerland has lately been taking energetic action for us, the dangers of the food situation cannot be sufficiently emphasized. Nothing would have a better influence in Vienna than the friendly behaviour of the Entente powers in regard to this. Even if Bohemia were willing to do more, it is unable to, since the Czech peasants are furnishing very little food for their own people.

2. *General Situation*

The continuous advance of the Czechs and the southern Slavs, especially the former, on to Austrian territory, has had a very depressing influence here. It cannot be understood why the Entente does not make clear its position whether it intends to accept at least some of Wilson's fourteen points, or none of them at all. What most worries us here, is that the Entente still refuses to have any direct communication with Austria. Even from the point of view of France herself, would it not be better if she

207

would let us know under what conditions she would agree to negotiate with Austria.

3

If a preliminary conference is impossible, because they do not want to take on any obligations before the peace negotiations (which, by the way, would not be the case in a conference that would be established purely with the aim of discussing the problems), such a conference should at least take place before the definite peace propositions are discussed in Paris, and it should give an opportunity to Austrians of all political parties to put forward their views. I believe that such a move, which is considered merely as an expedient, is absolutely necessary if at least even a partial compliance with justice is sought, and if a lasting peace is desired. It will be quite impossible to decide on the complicated questions of the states that are to be created out of the old Austro-Hungarian Empire without listening to the Austrians or the Hungarians, and without clearly seeing the possibilities of national settlement and the vital economic necessities of these new states, as well as their common interests created by nature and geography. However the Entente may base the frontiers of these future states within the late Austro-Hungarian territory on political reasons, the mutual economic interests of all these nations and states must also be remembered. In the first place, the payment and security of the Governmental debts of these two parts of the late Hapsburg monarchy—i.e. Austria and Hungary—should be dealt with; especially since the state insurance companies, the savings banks, the post office accounts, and so on, are all integrated with the safety of the enormous debts of the late constituent parts of Austria and Hungary. Without some joint organization the finances of all the new states built up on the late Austrian soil cannot be put on to a basis that will enable them to develop normally. That such an organization should be created for the Austrians and Germans also, who between them make up a population of twenty millions, is to the direct interest of the Entente states—especially France, which would greatly suffer from a complete collapse of Austrian finances. In the first place, the above-mentioned conference could be limited to dealing with the problem of the liquidation of common financial interests. A joint negotiation with regard to railways, riverine shipping and possible seaports, could also be carried out, since unless all these matters are put into order, any kind of economic organization in the new states will be impossible. This, again, could be followed by purely informative discussions about the future frontiers. I cannot sufficiently stress how important it seems to me, especially from the French point of view, to arrange a constructive policy for the financial situation of the late Austrian nations. The extremely serious economical and financial state of affairs that has been brought about in these nations does not seem to be sufficiently realized. In the interests of the economic re-establishment of the Western European states themselves, it is an unavoidable duty to look into this matter, all the more since the humiliations and economic burdens that the defeated powers will have to face can be made milder and less bitter just through such a friendly understanding in the economic sphere, and through that a really reconciliatory peace be established.

4

In regard to the question of the German Tyrol, I believe that it should be pointed out that it is in the interests of France herself that such an Italian expansion beyond the boundaries of the Italian language should not take place. This is so for purely strategical reasons, quite apart from the fact that to neglect such a basis and fundamental principle of the constitution of European states could not very well be reconciled with the other Italian claims for the Dalmatian coast. Neither can it be reconciled with the idea of a League of Nations and the creation of a lasting world peace.

On the day that I handed this memorandum to the French Ambassador he told me that he had news from Paris that France had not only given up her opposition to the sending of an international Commission to Berne for the investigation of Austria's needs, but that the members of the Commission would go on a special visit to Vienna. Hoover's two friends, Dr. Taylor and Captain Gregory, were the American representatives on the Commission, and M. Haguenin the French. A few more telegrams had to be exchanged with Versailles, and on December 31st, 1918, the members of the Inter-allied Commission drove to Buchs, to go on from there to Vienna.

When I arrived at Buchs on the morning of the New Year, Captain Gregory offered me a seat in their special train.

There was no dining-car on the train, but somehow an American cook prepared an improvised meal, which was served to me with the greatest possible kindness by two young American lieutenants.

When we left the mountainous regions and were traversing the beautiful Danubian plain, the first words of criticism against Austria were uttered. " This country could become a second Switzerland," said the Americans. " But first of all the cultivation of the soil would have to be intensified, so that it would be fifty times as fruitful as it is now. Let's hope that Austria will become a free, happy and self-sufficient state. It is Europe's duty to support with all its power this country that it has mutilated."

PART IV

CHAPTER I

THE few short years of the Socialist Government in Austria were full of parliamentary quarrels, financial disasters and social disorder. It proved an almost impossible task to keep alive the state after it had been dismembered. The new Austria, with a population of just over six million, was left with a capital in which dwelt more than a third of the inhabitants of the whole country. How was it to be fed? How was this town, that for practically half a millennium had been the centre and capital of South-Eastern Europe, to be administered?

The Socialist Government fell. But the Socialists remained in power in Vienna; and their achievements have to be admitted by all parties. No one can deny what they succeeded in doing for Vienna, for social and hygienic administration, for the population, whose work had to be completely reorganized. Their record is unequalled by that of almost any other municipal administration in the world. No wealthy city, unravaged by the war, has accomplished so much in the way of school hygiene and the care of children and expectant mothers. The man who took a leading part in this work was Professor Julius Tandler, who had been a pupil of my husband's and later his assistant, and who took his Chair.

But in other directions also Vienna proved itself strong enough to withstand the storms of fate that had raged over it. A new wave of artistic creation and thought developed in the midst of these first post-war years. Writers and poets of genius began to emerge. There was the young poet Franz Werfel, whose flaming songs of freedom spoke in the language

213

of the genius to the soul of martyred humanity. Now belief and faith in human progress was needed, and it was found in the strong will to save Austria, not as a political Empire, but an empire of culture, art and civilization for the whole world.

Towards the end of 1919 Hugo von Hoffmannsthal had called on me and spoken about the necessity of keeping Austria as a cultural centre. He said: " My dear friend, Austria's unique culture must be saved. We want to take Salzburg and raise Mozart and the town of his birth to a truly Austrian symbol of artistic creation. I have discussed this with Max Reinhardt, and we both agreed that even if the state is politically shattered, its soul must be eternal. And you must help us in our project. . . ."

And he developed the idea of the Salzburg Festivals. He was optimistic in his absolute conviction that that day would come when Austria would prove to the world that she is undefeatable. " Believe me," he said, " the whole world will come to Salzburg, will admire the mountain peaks bathed in glowing light, and will be overwhelmed by the art that has been created and is to be created in that Alpine wonderland. The victors will come on a pilgrimage to defeated Austria— whose civilization has remained victorious."

Of course I was delighted with this idea. I remembered Ilg, my late teacher, and his fight for true Austrian art, when he wrote about the beauty of the Baroque as a true expression of Austrian nature. And from what I could gather from my talks with Max Reinhardt and Hugo von Hoffmannsthal about the preparations for Salzburg, it was to a Renaissance of the Baroque. I was proud and happy to have been asked to write a message of greeting for the first number of the Salzburg Festival paper. And I should like to reprint it now—when there is no more Austria, and when Salzburg has lost the spirit of its great initiators, Reinhardt and von Hoffmannsthal.

"The Beginning"

A word on the Mozart Festspielhaus at Salzburg.

A state has been overthrown. A throne has fallen. A people has been torn to pieces. A new kind of state has been welded together. A new world order has begun. Nothing has remained as it was.

And what has been the first thing to be born of this chaos?

The Mozart Festival at Salzburg. A temple of divine art. A symbol of indestructible Austrian culture. A confession of faith by Austria.

The beginning.

Before uncertainty, pain, and disaster have been suppressed, before individuals have started to rebuild their own lives, before the question of the actual existence of the nation has been solved, people have come together with one desire—to build a holy temple of art on the spot where Mozart was born, for his eternal memory and for a confirmation of his nation's indestructibility.

Salzburg, whose surroundings breathe a hidden southern charm, Salzburg in whose art the Gothic and the Baroque have united in such powerful beauty, Salzburg in whose beautifully circumscribed yet open valley was cradled that genius of music, Amadeus Mozart.

Through its symbol Mozart, Austrian culture should develop the full richness of its nature. Not only music, but the genius of speech also should bear witness to the invincible values of the soul. From Calderon to Raimund we should have a true spiritual League of Nations. Here it should grow, on Austrian soil. Here it should stand, the meeting-place of international art. Faithfully it should fulfil the task set to it by nature— to communicate and distribute the true values of the human soul, from north to south, from east to west. That should be Salzburg's mission.

Everyone should, according to their limitations, contribute something to the building of this great temple of culture. And everyone who can give, must give as much as possible, in order to realize the dream of a true church where, after this long and dreadful time of hatred, men of all nations should be united in the worship of art.

Remember—one day history will relate that when Austria had fallen to pieces, when the little newly-born republic was having to fight a despairing struggle for its very existence, when Vienna was in the grip of hatred and faced with an uncertain future, when all Europe was in a turmoil, without time to care for art and beauty, the men and women of little Austria tried to find a way out. But they did not attempt, as the more practical nations did, to concentrate upon the urgent economic questions. They concentrated upon the one thing that neither war nor disaster had been able to destroy in their souls—Art. And they set about creating the Salzburg Festival, as a symbol of their beliefs.

So, in years to come, it will be said : This was the first smile of the world after its disaster.

It was the beginning!

So, Salzburg came into existence—at first only with the most modest means. After incessant attempts to raise money the first season was opened. As yet there was no Festspielhaus. But Max Reinhardt's genius had transformed a lack into an advantage. The Domplatz in front of Salzburg Cathedral was turned into the most beautiful stage in Europe. Mountains were its back-cloth, and church spires were part of its scenery. The light of the setting sun furnished an illumination that could not have been equalled by the most wonderful electrical equipment.

The actors did not wait behind the scenes to appear on the stage. I shall never forget the first performance of *Jederman*, when the incomparable Moissi was sitting in the front row of the audience, wrapped in a dark coat, his remarkable pale face turned towards the great stage; when his cue came he stood up, threw off his coat, and walked straight on to the scene. This in no way diminished the magnificent theatricality of the whole performance, but seemed actually to heighten it. And his sweet and compelling voice sounded even stronger and more lovely in the open.

Later on, when the Festspielhaus had become a reality, and in it the greatest musical artists were creating, one of the most prominent singers was bound to me by rather special ties. He was Richard Mayr, who had once studied medicine and been a pupil of my husband's. I remember Emil coming home one night and speaking enthusiastically to me about the voice of a young man who had sung so beautifully at a students' meeting that all the others had stopped to listen to him. My husband spoke to the boy, and advised him right away to give up medicine and become a singer. Because, though he *might* have become a good doctor and helped humanity by it, it was *certain* that he would become a great singer, and help humanity in that way. Richard Mayr had followed this advice, and at the time of the first Salzburg Festival he was one of the leading European singers.

Egon Friedell, the great historian, was collaborating with Max Reinhardt. Oscar Strnad, the brilliant architect, who had brought about a renaissance in the theatre, was creating the background for all this abundance of art. But the unification of these different individualities and arts into a single master-piece was the accomplishment of the personality of Max Reinhardt.

Max Reinhardt, internationally recognized as a genius, had put all his energies into the creation of Salzburg. He bought " Leopoldskron ", a seventeenth-century castle near Salzburg, built by Fischer von Erlach, and had it completely decorated and reconstructed in the style of its period. There he gave little private performances for his friends, and I have spent some very happy days there, enjoying the wonderful harmony of production, acting, and décor. But in Salzburg Max Reinhardt still remained true to his internationalism. His achievements for the French drama, from Molière to the newest unknown dramatist, were unequalled. His true understanding of France, and love for that country, may best be shown by reproducing some extracts from a letter that he wrote me much later.

Salzburg, July 28th, 1937.

. . . We have seen more of the wonderful Exposition. The whole thing is a grandiose " documentation " of the genius of France. We have been driving round the country again, for another four days, and have seen Gothic cathedrals, castles, gardens, Rococo furniture; we have wandered with delight amongst the almost overwhelming profusion of French sculpture; we have marvelled at the unequalled wonders of the lighting in Paris, and stood at the memorial to the Unknown Soldier—this greatest and most simple monument in the world. (The idea itself already has become eternal, and with it a new chapter of the revolution has begun.) Then, when one returns to a nearby hotel, one can't help saying to oneself, " This people's creative power is unequalled." And once again one falls in love with her perpetually young, perpetually exciting beauty. And she will be the one to laugh last, even though her waiters and taxi-drivers are on strike. . . .

While we were driving through Switzerland (where the waiters who were not on strike served us with disgusting food) an idea came into my head. I would like to tell it to you, before this year's " Festspiel-excitement ", which is greater than ever before, floods everything else.

The greatest accomplishment of French genius was, and still is, the French Revolution. It is not over, it still lingers on; it has developed into the World Revolution. . . . Before it began (1789) the clear fanfare of *Figaro* sounded out. In my opinion France could not find a more triumphant, a more significant and also a more attractive way of opening the theatre of the Exposition than by a representation of her Revolution.

The text is already there. One of our greatest contemporaries, Romain Rolland, has dedicated the main part of his work to a dramatic representation of the Revolution. He has written a cycle in no less than seven volumes. I know them very well. . . . With the help of Romain Rolland a marvellous drama could be constructed in quite short time, that would begin with the taking of the Bastille and end with the deaths of Danton and Robespierre. This drama would deal also with the fate of the King and Queen, which up to now have not been dealt with in any of the dramas of the Revolution that I know about. But it seems to me to be a matter of course that the fall of the monarchy marked a decisive phase of the Revolution, and the whole theme would be enormously enriched by it, becoming more colourful, more dramatic. . . .

Where in the world, or even in the history of the world, could be found another drama with such an abundance of marvellous, sharply defined roles as that of the French Revolution, which really *suffered* from an over-abundance of strong personalities, and perhaps just because of it had to fail. . . .

. . . We are really looking forward to seeing you soon as our guest at Leopoldskron.

With best wishes from my wife also, I am your sincerely devoted

MAX REINHARDT.

CHAPTER II

Even after its downfall Austria remained a centre of international ambitions and intrigues. This can be shown by extracts from interviews in Vienna with the French, German and Italian ambassadors. These had been written down immediately after they had taken place, and so give an entirely faithful account of the interviews.

The aspirations and ambitions of her neighbours were centred on Austria, and all their political gambles had Austria in view as a principal stake.

INTERVIEW WITH ITALIAN AMBASSADOR, SIGNOR ORSINI, October 2nd, 1922

Signor Orsini, who is usually a very quiet and even phlegmatic man, was most upset. He declared—Italy won't let herself be turned out of Austria, and she is determined to take the strictest precautions to maintain her position in this country. She would not allow Benes to become the ruler of Central Europe. Italy would even prefer to take up arms than quietly stand aside and watch Austria become a dependency of Yugoslavia and Czechoslovakia. Signor Orsini complained bitterly about England's behaviour, because they obviously want completely to remove Italy from Austria. But that would mean a great danger to the peace of Europe, because Italy would never permit it.

Signor Orsini also explained to me the reasons for the bad relations between England and Italy. He said that the English Prime Minister, Lloyd George, had invited Schanzer, the Italian Minister of Foreign Affairs, to come and see him in London in order to discuss some important problems. (I learned from the French side, that the question was concerned with the Anglo-Italian treaty of alliance.) Schanzer came to London as arranged, but was not received by Lloyd George, although he waited for five days for Lloyd George to fix the date for a conference. After these five days had passed the Italian Foreign Minister returned home, very hurt. And this offence against Schanzer, which very soon became common property amongst Italian political circles, stirred up public opinion there against England. . . .

INTERVIEW WITH THE FRENCH AMBASSADOR, M. LEFEVRE PONTALIS, December 7th, 1922

The French Ambassador made some really astounding statements, and gave a lecture for nearly an hour on the history of Geneva. To give a short résumé, the story, according to Lefevre, is as follows:

In July of this year great Fascist demonstrations took place at Bellincona, in the canton of Tessin. These had carefully been prepared by prolonged agitation, and began to assume proportions that disquietened the Swiss Government. At the same time an agitation had been developing in the Austrian Vorarlberg, with the aim of reviving the movement in favour of an "Anschluss" of Vorarlberg with Switzerland. During this time the Swiss Government had been subject to cautious inquiries from the Italian side, asking if they would be willing, in the case of a dividing up of Austria, to include the Vorarlberg into their territory. In addition to that, Italy approached other powers with the suggestion that a commission of control should be established over Austria, which would not have its seat in that country, but outside it, with an Italian president at its head who would have practically unlimited powers. It was quite obvious that here one was dealing with a well-thought-out Italian plan.

In the meantime the situation within Austria had been deteriorating, and when, in August, Lloyd George had declined an English guarantee for an Austrian loan, the downfall of Austria seemed certain. Negotiations commenced between England and Italy on the fate of Austria. And Italy's aspirations began to show forth more and more clearly. In Austria itself, especially in the Alpine provinces, a strong party had grown up which worked for a close connection between Italy and Austria. The Landeshauptmann of Styria—Rintelen—approached the English Ambassador in Vienna, and asked him to discuss the following idea with Orsini, the Italian Ambassador: Austria's downfall was unavoidable. In such a case Styria could not possibly exist on its own, as it only produced enough foodstuff to feed its population for two months of the year. In no circumstances whatsoever would Styria agree to entering into close connection with Yugoslavia. On the other hand, Italy as well as Styria would derive great advantages from a close collaboration. Styria could furnish Italy with iron and timber, and Italy could furnish food in return. Similar tendencies are becoming apparent in Tyrol and Carinthia, tendencies that find a strong support in Italy. In the Tyrol a slogan was put forward demanding the addition of northern Tyrol to Italy, in order to create a unified Tyrolese country in which they would thus become united with their brethren of the southern Tyrol.

This was the situation when M. Lefevre went to Seipel to tell him that he was going to Marienbad for a cure. The French Ambassador put the questions to the Bundeschancellor Seipel, whether he could go there in peace, and whether there were not important developments shortly to be foreseen. Dr. Seipel told M. Lefevre that he could leave Vienna with perfect confidence.

Only eight days later the French Ambassador learned that Dr. Seipel intended to go to Prague, Berlin and Rome. M. Lefevre did not interrupt his cure, but when he returned from Marienbad he went to the Bundeschancellor and reminded him of his assurance that nothing important would happen in Austria in the course of the next few weeks. To that Dr. Seipel answered: " The journey to Prague and Berlin certainly had nothing in it that would be likely to interest the French." M. Lefevre then said: " But you went to Verona also, and there other plans seemed to have been discussed that are likely to disquiet the whole of Europe." Dr. Seipel said that this was perfectly correct, but he had been by no means willing to let a third person know about it. M. Lefevre accepted this, but, he added, he had complete information about the Verona negotiations, which had dealt with what was practically the inclusion of Austria in Italy. He warned Dr. Seipel against proceeding in this way before he once more tried the methods that had already been used, and had, for some incomprehensible reason been given up—i.e. the League of Nations. The Bundeschancellor did not at all agree with this point since Austria's experiences with the League last year had proved its unwillingness to help when help was really needed and Austria could not possibly rely on it, or risk anything on its account. M. Lefevre insisted that it should be tried once again, because otherwise a serious European conflagration might result.

Switzerland also had heard about this Italian scheme, and had vigorously protested against it. The scheme was to make an independent Alpine state out of the Tyrol, Carinthia, and Styria, under an Italian Protectorate—so that the route from Switzerland to Hungary would also come under Italian domination. Italy would have drawn into its sphere of power the whole of the communications between Western and Eastern Europe. The Swiss Ambassador had repeated long talks with M. Lefevre, in the course of which he declared that Switzerland would fight against the execution of such a plan. Up to this time Switzerland had four neighbouring states and she wanted it to remain so; she did not want to have three neighbours, two of which—Germany and Italy—would circumscribe and threaten her. The Swiss Government was negotiating with other powers also, to make this Italian plan impossible; and it was the Swiss Government that was urging the League of Nations to take up the work of Austrian assistance again with the utmost promptness and energy. The idea of assistance for Austria being carried out within the frame of the League of Nations thus began to become a reality. M. Lefevre once more interviewed Dr. Seipel, to whom he explained that the action was not to be taken by the League of Nations as such, but as an action within the framework of the League : and that if Austria tried to prevent such an action she would be shouldering a dreadful responsibility. Finally, Dr. Seipel declared that he was ready to make an approach again, and Herr Gruenberger, the Minister of Foreign Affairs, and Graf Mensdorff, were sent to Geneva.

The affair did not progress there, so once again M. Lefevre called upon Dr. Seipel, and explained to him that this very complex and important question should be acted upon with more energy, and it would be very useful if the Bundeschancellor himself would go to Geneva. Thereupon Dr. Seipel told M. Lefevre that he had just received the message from Herr Eichhof, the Austrian Minister at Paris, that he had been asked to call on the French Minister of Foreign Affairs, and that he had been told it was the earnest wish of the French Government that the Bundeschancellor himself personally should go to Geneva, in order to force the machinery of the League of Nations to work more quickly. Influenced by this demand the Bundeschancellor determined to go to Geneva. But he openly declared that if the League of Nations once more did not succeed in carrying out its task, he would prefer Rome ten times more than Prague. . . .

On the same night Dr. Seipel called a meeting of the Ministers at which, after long struggles—especially with the German nationalists who opposed him at the beginning—it was decided that he should go to Geneva. And it was soon proved that the opinion which France had always held—that only the League of Nations was able to accomplish the salvation of Austria—was perfectly correct. Now the task at Geneva has been accomplished; Dr. Seipel carried through the decisions that had been taken there with admirable intelligence and energy. However, since Mussolini had come to power in Italy in the meantime, the plan for the creation of an Alpine state once more had been taken up; and he said that he knew certain circles in Austria were even more strongly sympathetic to it now than before just because of this Fascist victory. On account of all this one had to keep one's eyes open, and one could never guess what was going to happen next.

INTERVIEW WITH ITALIAN AMBASSADOR, SIGNOR ORSINI, September 4th, 1923

The Italian Ambassador . . . who had returned from Rome yesterday, categorically declared, "Italy has no intention of conquest." Shortly before he left Rome he had spoken to Signor Mussolini, and the latter had made this statement to him : " I am not going to have an Imperialist policy. I do not think about conquests, but I do not want to fall into traps that may be laid for me. I conduct Italy's foreign policy, and I do not intend to share this leadership, or have it taken out of my hands either by the League of Nations, or any other such body."

INTERVIEW WITH THE GERMAN AMBASSADOR, DR. PFEIFFER, December 14th, 1922

. . . The German Ambassador also spoke to me about the history of the Geneva Conference. He said that on the 12th or 13th of August he had called on the Bundeschancellor, Dr. Seipel, and that Vice-Chancellor Frank also had been present at their interview. The situation seemed absolutely hopeless at this time, and Dr. Pfeiffer had been asked what would be the German reaction if Austria would declare in favour of an " Anschluss ". The German Ambassador answered that as a matter of course it could be taken that if Austria was to come to Germany it would be received with open arms. He had to point out, though, that both the peace treaties of St. Germain and of Versailles included paragraphs about the preliminaries that would have to take place before an Anschluss could be brought about. Austria would have to ask permission from the League of Nations for the Anschluss. Now there was the question of how the Austrian state would announce such an intention—would it be on the wide basis of a plebiscite, or would it be sufficient for the national assembly, as the representatives of the Austrian people, to announce such a step. The German Ambassador spoke about the consequences that would arise from such a step. It might end well for Austria. But it seemed obvious to him that if France was to consent to it, she would also demand from the League the decision that the left side of the Rhine, and Westphalia . . . should be separated from Germany. But if the action was not successful there was the possibility that in such a case Yugoslavia and Czechoslovakia would march in with their troops. To which Vice-Chancellor Frank said : " We realize this, but we are convinced that Germany would take over the defence of the Austrian frontiers."

The Ambassador : " With our 86,000 men? "

Frank : " But there are your civilian fighting organizations."

The Ambassador : " They aren't very reliable. They would go home if it got too cold."

At this moment a telegram from Franckenstein, the Austrian Minister in London, was handed in. It stated that the Entente Powers had decided to submit the Austrian question to the League of Nations, as they no longer regarded it as a purely economic problem, but one of politics. This problem should not only be negotiated through a Commission but should be put before the whole Committee of the League of Nations.

Thereupon the German Ambassador said to the Bundeschancellor, " Well, your Excellency, you will have to make an independent decision now."

The following day Dr. Seipel said to the Ambassador that he would follow his advice, but he did not tell him of his projected visit to Italy.

If the Anschluss had been brought about at this time Austria could not have got much support from Germany, either morally or through its political or economic lead. A picture of the hopeless disorder and disorganization in the Reich during 1923 is given by the following record of interviews with the German Ambassador.

CONVERSATION WITH THE GERMAN AMBASSADOR, *January 17th, 1923*

Dr. Pfeiffer, the German Ambassador, described the position of Germany to me as being almost desperate. The state of affairs in Bavaria was very critical, and a civil war might break out any time. It should not be overlooked that the National Socialists are in no way identical with the " Heimwehr ". The National Socialists, who are the most radical party, received a great increase of strength by the addition of the Clericals, as well as the " Alldeutsch " of the so-called middle party. Who is behind the workings of the National Socialists no one knows so far, but the official leader, the Austrian, Hitler, is nothing but a puppet. At the same time Bavaria is threatened by a " putsch " of the Communists, which, it is said, will precede an advance of the National Socialists. The position in the Reich is horrible too. The slogan of a united national front cannot be carried out, because there is no united front possible between men who are hungry and those who are satiated. The people of the Right understand a united front to be a union of all parties to restore the status quo—if possible under an Emperor. And those of the Left see a united front as a far-reaching policy of socialization, and a through repression of reaction, as well as common action with other parties abroad who have an internationalist standpoint. Dr. Pfeiffer thinks that Germany will soon have to face an atrocious food crisis, as the potato crop—though it is of the best quality—is the smallest for a long time. There is not sufficient corn either. As well as this, transport difficulties are increasing because of the sequestration of the Ruhr coal. Altogether he is most pessimistic about the future development of affairs; but he adds that all this had not only been foreseen by Herr von Rosenberg, but even wished for by him, as he thinks that above all Germany must be freed from the treaty of Versailles. If the French take energetic measures, then, at last, the Germans will become one nation. Dr. Pfeiffer expressed his doubts as to whether this view of Dr. Rosenberg will prove to be correct in the future.

CONVERSATION WITH THE GERMAN AMBASSADOR, *November 17th, 1923.*

The German Ambassador arrived in Vienna yesterday from Munich. In the conversation that he had with me to-day he described the drastic situation that exists in Munich. Nowadays the Jews are being persecuted there, as well as the Catholics. Cardinal Faulhaber, who had openly spoken against Hitler, has been threatened with death. The traitors Ludendorff, Hitler, and Ehrhardt go freely about the town, and everywhere they are cheered. Neither their imprisonment or even bringing them before a court is thought about. On the Government offices only the black-white-red and the blue-white flags are hung out; not a single red-black-gold flag can be seen in Bavaria. At the moment the most powerful person in Munich is Ehrhardt. The nationalists are split. Those who have Hitler as their leader want to retain the unity of the German Reich, with Hitler as Reichs-Chancellor; others want to set up an independent National-Socialist Republic in Bavaria; a third set, with Kahr at their head, want to reintroduce the Monarchy, and have chosen the rather confused and undistinguished slogan, " True to the Reich and true to Bavaria ". A fourth lot want to march on Berlin and there put an end to Marxism. In short, there is an indescribable muddle everywhere. Rather significant in view of the situation, is the fact that the Munich students assaulted their Rector and threw him out of the University buildings, and that he, who is the highest official in the University, had humbly to ask permission of the students in order to re-enter the University building; and he only received their consent after he had declared that he was proud of the fact that his son was a follower of Hitler.

Dr. Pfeiffer described Munich as a gigantic lunatic asylum. The Reich Government was unable to do anything in Bavaria. Dr. Pfeiffer declared that it was very lucky that the " putsch " broke out sooner than it was intended. For Hitler is understood to have had the plan of marching with his regiment of three thousand men against the French. That would have brought about a real catastrophe, as the French would have bombed the city.

Then the German Ambassador proceeded to discuss the situation in the Reich itself. He declared that no one could possibly foresee what would come from the future. It was possible that the Stresemann Cabinet would remain in power, although things were very difficult for Dr. Stresemann, since almost half of his own party are against him. It was possible that the German Nationalists might enter into the Government and thus bring about a majority of the Right. Finally there is the possibility that a Government will not be formed at all, and General Seeckt might become dictator. In Dr. Pfeiffer's opinion, a dissolution of the Reichstag is out of the question. The German Ambassador believes that General Seeckt is a true friend of the Republic who has not allowed the Reichswehr to become entangled with politics. Up to now he has brilliantly fulfilled his duties.

Not only was the German Government now powerless in Bavaria against Kahr and Hitler, but in the Rhine and Ruhr districts as well, it lacked authority against the Stinnes, the Otto Wolffs and their like. These people are at present the real rulers of those districts, and as they would prefer to go over to France, because it would mean that they would not have to pay any more new taxes, it might be expected that one of these days a new Rhine-Republic independent of Prussia would be formed. A similar situation is also to be found in Hanover. There, too, a strong desire is growing for independence from Prussia. In fact, it is unlikely that a dissolution of Prussia can be avoided.

At the end of our interview Dr. Pfeiffer spoke about Germany's dreadful financial situation. He believed that only a really big international loan could help them. And he thinks that America and England would be willing to give Germany credits if France were to change her policy towards Germany. France would be willing to do this provided that England and America freed her from the repayment of the debts she owed them. But the two powers refused to do so. Because of all this Dr. Pfeiffer thought that Germany's future was absolutely uncertain and unpredictable.

CHAPTER III

It is beyond the limits of this book to attempt a description of Ignaz Seipel, the Austrian Bundeschancellor. That belongs to the chapters of world history. But I would like to point out that, in my opinion, this man's strength, which had succeeded finally in saving Austria from the hopeless situation brought about by the Peace of St. Germain, which had brought order into the chaos of this unbalanced little state, might have saved Austria from its final and complete disaster of March 1938. Had this man lived, Austria might not be dead to-day.

At the time when I first met Dr. Seipel, Zimmermann, the General Commissioner for Austria appointed by the League of Nations, was ruling over the country. It was a difficult time. Every Austrian initiative was stifled, forbidden and suppressed. Things could not go on like this. If it was desired to give new confidence to the people of this little country, such a shameful form of foreign control would have to be abolished.

Ignaz Seipel and his Minister of Foreign Affairs intended to inform France—not, however, through the usual diplomatic channels—how intolerable was this form of foreign supervision over an " independent state ", and how it was degrading the desired and proclaimed " independence " to a tasteless joke. It was this situation that was driving Austria towards an Anschluss.

I was asked to the Ballhausplatz, and greeted by Dr. Mataja (the Foreign Minister) with the words : " You must again help with some wire-pulling and work behind the scenes. To begin with, are you free to go to Paris? . . ."

A few days later I was sitting opposite my best friend, Paul Painlevé, who was then Premier of France.

Whatever profession he had adopted, Painlevé would have risen to its head. He was a universal genius, with unlimited

PAUL PAINLEVÉ

creative abilities. Higher mathematics, the most abstract of all the sciences, was his true field of thought—a field which he shared with Henri Poincaré and Einstein. But he never permitted his preoccupation with these lofty regions of human thought to isolate him from the world.

When he was ten his tutors said that he was perfectly ready for a university education. His precocious intelligence has been compared with that of a d'Alembert, a Pascal, or a Newton. He was still only a student when his discoveries in the field of mathematics, mechanics, and astronomy became famous. Henri Poincaré once said of him: "I wanted to call out to Painlevé—Stop! You have started on a road that leads to an insurmountable wall. Well, our youngest colleague came to this wall, and with an almost miraculous strength he succeeded in jumping over it. His triumph is one of the greatest triumphs of French science."

But, unlike most of his colleagues, it was not enough for him to wander upon the lonely heights of thought. Once, when he was engaged in a serious struggle in the Chamber of Deputies during his term as Premier, I asked him why he had left the peaceful, silent realm of science for the stormy and uncertain world of politics. He answered: "I spent so much of my life in those lofty regions that I began to feel lonely. It is cold up there, and one day I dared to jump down into ordinary life. I was longing for action. I wanted to replace the word by the deed."

A long time before the war Painlevé had concerned himself with the problem of flying, and he was one of the practical as well as the theoretical initiators of the aeroplane. Together with William Wright and Henri Farman he held for some months the long-distance flight record. The world laughed at him then when he prophesied the important role that the aeroplane was bound to play in the next war. But he did not abandon his belief and the first Government financial measure for flying was forced through Parliament by him.

Painlevé, lover and worker for peace, had, like that other

apostle of peace, Berthelot, created a dreadful new weapon of war by his improvements in the technique of flying. But, unlike Goethe's sorcerer who complained "The ghosts I call up I cannot make to disappear," he realized the dangers inherent in this blessing of mankind and attempted to change the evil ghosts into good ones. This he wanted to do by trying to internationalize European flying. In 1931 he declared: "In the course of the last few months we have been studying a new method of internationalizing European flying. . . . Twenty-five years ago I was a protagonist of flying when as yet it was only in its infancy. At that time my greatest wish was that this achievement of the human mind which had succeeded in breaking that most burdensome fetter of humanity—the law of gravitation—would some day overcome the burden of human hatred by bringing all nations closer to each other. Since then I have received angry letters in which I have been reproached that this invention serves to kill helpless people, women and children. I thought that it must be left to time alone to put an end to this dreadful threat . . . once the aeroplane has succeeded in overcoming this barrier it will become a means of bringing about a mutual reconciliation amongst the nations."

Perhaps this dream of his may seem laughable to-day in view of an international situation that is more threatening than ever. He is dead now, and his idea may seem the impossible vision of an idealist. But this is always the case when logic wants to cash its post-dated cheques. In the long run, though perhaps not until centuries have passed, an idealist of the stature of Painlevé is always proved to be right. There must come a time when his dream will be realized.

As an Admiralty expert before the war, Painlevé had written memoranda about the danger of submarines. And when the war broke out this scientist became one of the leaders of his nation; he became a tireless organizer, an orator whose powers of speech could be compared only with those of a Danton. And he proved his physical courage beyond any doubt when, in 1920, he undertook the dangerous flight from Canton to Hanoi, and again in 1925, when he was War Minister and he flew to Morocco to suppress the rebellion there.

Courage was the most prominent feature of his character. An unconscious, uncalculating courage, absolute equanimity in the face of all danger.

Was it not natural that this man, who had taken for his own Michelet's motto *" que la France déclare la paix au monde "*, should faithfully carry out the Locarno policy, in company with Briand? Was it not natural that a man who believed in justice above everything, should be strongly moved by the fate of Austria? Painlevé knew the Austrian soul. He loved Austria, whose culture he had long admired. As I have already mentioned, he was deeply interested in music and he came to Vienna, led by his love for Mahler's work.

I was one of the first Austrians allowed to visit Paris after the war. One of the personal friends whom I most wanted to see was Painlevé. I found him unchanged—still my friend. He was moved by the fate of my country. He had wished to fight for a policy that attempted to help Austria.

" I will do whatever lies in my power, I promise you that I will help your country to guard its independence, and I want to see that every possibility for giving life to this new but weakened nation should be created. I will carry out what I regard in the truest sense of the word as my mission and my highest duty." This he said when I saw him for the first time after our long separation by the war.

And he used every opportunity to keep his promise with untiring zeal. He took the decisive lead when the League of Nations was induced to guarantee the first big loan to Austria.

So it was natural that I should have found a willing ear when, after my interview with Dr. Seipel and Dr. Mataja, I came to Paris to explain the intolerable position that had been brought about in Austria by the General Commissioner. Of course Painlevé had been informed through the official diplomatic channels of Austria's ardent wish to be freed from its chains. But I was able to state the position in a different way, and show how it was working out in the ordinary incidents of everyday life. And so the French Premier promised me to declare at the next Session of the League that the powers must make an end to the situation.

On September 8th, 1925, Painlevé spoke in Geneva, demanding the instantaneous recall of the Commissioner, Zimmermann, from Austria. And all the protests and all the intrigues were put to an end by his wonderful and convincing declaration that had helped to bring victory to a just cause.

Less than a year later, in June 1926, Dr. Seipel wanted to go to Paris in order to express his thanks and gratitude personally. At this time Painlevé was no longer Premier but Minister of War.

I was in Paris during Dr. Seipel's stay there. Painlevé told me, " If I go out of my way to show an unusual regard for the Austrian Chancellor, I will be doing it first and foremost to show my esteem for such a great man. But also I will be doing it in order once and for all to declare openly my attitude towards Austria. In my opinion Austria is the focus of the whole of Central Europe. This is not sufficiently realized in France. And because of it we may have to face some unpleasant surprises. Seipel is a great statesman and he must succeed in forming some kind of Danubian federation eventually. If this doesn't happen, then we will have new European upsets."

As it is never possible openly to declare the reasons for the political visit of the head of a state to another country a pretext had to be found for Dr. Seipel's journey to Paris. And so he gave a lecture at the Sorbonne—to an audience of twelve hundred listeners. He spoke in French, and the theme chosen after consultation with Painlevé, was " The true face of Austria ". It was a philosophic address on the characteristics of the Austrians. At the end of the lecture there was a brilliant official reception given by the Minister of War.

The guests at the reception typified Painlevé's double role

as a leading politician and one of the greatest scientists of his time. Diplomats and politicians, scientists and artists, were equally represented at the reception. The invitations announced *" Une heure de musique "*. Maria Freund sang Ravel's " Melodie grecque ", and when the composer entered the room he was greeted by loud applause. Seipel, who was sitting next to the great French poetess, Comtesse de Noailles, and who did not know the composer by sight, asked her what was the cause of this ovation. When she told him, Seipel went over to Ravel when the recital had finished and said how very much he had liked his composition " Vienna ", both for its music and its title.

" I should like the first performance of my arrangements of the Johann Strauss waltzes to be in Vienna," said Ravel. " For that is the place where this Austro-French music should first be heard."

The rooms emptied slowly, but Ravel and the Comtesse de Noailles were deep in discussion and noticed nothing, even when they began putting some of the lights out.

Ravel said : " I say, although I am an internationalist, that art must be national. I am writing purely French music. I want to go on writing purely French music."

" Yes," answered the Comtesse de Noailles, " but it does not lie within your power to exclude the super-national element from your work. It does not lie within the powers of any creative artist to omit from his work that which belongs to the whole of mankind in common. . . ."

Painlevé, who had been listening quietly, interrupted her. " I was just thinking about a saying of Leibniz : *' Pouvoir penser inconsciemment en nombre est le bonheur le plus divin! ' "*

" What a marvellous sentence," exclaimed Ravel. " Isn't music also the mathematical expression of thought? "

" Not all music," Madame de Noailles protested. " You must exclude Wagner from this category. And just now Paul Valéry said to me that he recognizes one musician only—

235

Wagner. But, be that as it may, one should avoid people who do not love music. As Shakespeare said : ' Fear the heart that does not love music.' "

My sister, Sofie Clémenceau, who had joined the group, asked : " But can a man who only cares for one composer love music at all? "

Turning to Seipel, who had remained silent right through the discussion, Painlevé said : " People who don't love music have no feeling. They could not understand an evening such as this, which was the expression of a complete and undisturbed harmony. I hope this harmony will continue."

More than two years after this visit to Paris Dr. Seipel told me that he would very much like to invite Painlevé to visit Vienna. " But it will be necessary to find an unpolitical pretext for it," he said. " I should like to be allowed to greet the great scientist instead of the great statesman. And that would be the only possibility for his acceptance of our invitation."

To find such a pretext was not easy, as can be seen by the following letter that Dr. Seipel wrote me.

Hütteldorf, July 25th, 1928.

MY DEAR FRAU HOFRAT ZUCKERKANDL,

The last months' sharp and exhausting parliamentary and foreign political campaigns made it impossible for me to see you. Now, when I wanted to ask you to call on me again, I understand that you have gone to Bad Gastein.

A worthy invitation for M. Painlevé to come to Vienna is just as much on my mind as it is on yours. But unfortunately I have not yet found a pretext for giving such an invitation. I have tried again and again to decide what organization could officially send the invitation. But every one of them seems too small and too unimportant for it. The Government itself is out of the question of course, as there is no reason whatsoever why the French Minister of War should come to Vienna. I will call at the

Academy of Science again, where, as I have already told you in confidence, the necessary enthusiasm is still lacking. Once M. Painlevé is here, on a good pretext, of course the Government will not fail to honour him as he deserves. Our Minister Gruenberger never fails to let a single occasion pass when he could remind me of this matter.

I wish you a pleasant stay in Bad Gastein and a success for your cure.

With the heartiest greetings, I am always yours,

SEIPEL.

However, a pretext was eventually found, and Painlevé came to Vienna. He was received with all due honour and all the official festivities appropriate to such an important visit.

But when he said good-bye to me he remarked, " In spite of everything that has happened here, the strange magic that seems to enchant this town is as strong as ever. The people here are different from anywhere else. These Viennese men and women have something of the marvellous unconsciousness of a child. What especially touches me is what I should like to call the ingenuous simplicity of their character. This is what I consider to be the real characteristic of the Viennese nature. I have travelled much and have encountered many brilliant people from many countries. But nowhere else have I found this civilized frankness, this quiet smile. It is the smile of a nation embued with an ancient culture and great traditions."

CHAPTER IV

EVER since the war Austria had been weak and needed friends who were great and powerful in order to live again. How wonderfully the prophetic words uttered by my father more than half a century ago had come true. He had said : " The true fate of Austria is bound up with the Western democracies, and their great men will be the men who are important for Austria's fate."

My highest duty was to try to execute my father's spiritual testament. And it made me very happy that, after the horrors of the war were over, my sister was able to be my most faithful collaborator in this task. She took every opportunity of giving both political and humanitarian help to Austria. And it was a true happiness for her that her husband, Paul Clémenceau, was able and willing to assist her work of love and faith in a truly chivalrous spirit.

President Edouard Herriot was another energetic friend of Austria. With the utmost far-sightedness he had realized earlier than most of his contemporaries how important was this little state, and from the very beginning he had intervened in a helpful and friendly way whenever he could be of any assistance in building her up.

It was my good luck to be on very friendly terms with the Comtesse Anne de Noailles, who had worked with real devotion for many years to bring about a political rapprochement between London, Paris and Vienna. She had the talents of a real statesman, all the charm of a delightful woman and the gifts of a great poet. Her influence was enormous. She was a friend of Briand, Caillaux, Painlevé and almost all the influential people of her time. And as she was also a friend of mine and of Austria, I should like to give a description of this woman who meant so much to me.

The Comtesse Anne de Noailles was fifty-three years old when she died in May 1933—the greatest lyric poet that France had produced during her lifetime. "The Noailles," as she was known in Paris, lived in the heart of the nation that had kept alive its interest in poetry even in these days of its neglect. France is the country where verse is still read.

But these lines are not intended as a valuation of her poetic work, they are concerned with her personality. But even here, the light of inquiry will only expose the most obvious of her characteristics, for this wonderful, this really exceptional woman never really disclosed herself to the world around her. Like a skilful painter whose strength is greatest in his powers of elimination, the Noailles kept hidden within herself the details that made up her personality. She only gave away the intense passion of her heart in some of her almost bacchantic verses. Anne de Noailles had sprung from a noble Rumanian family. She was a Brancovan, heiress of the Greek and Rumanian strains of the Mavrocordatos and the Bibescos. But she had been born and brought up in Paris. Her father had died only too early. Her beautiful mother had been surrounded by interesting people of an international circle of society. In her nursery she lived a life made banal by governesses. But in the soul of this young girl poetry throve, uninfluenced by her surroundings. In 1901, at the age of eighteen, she had already published her first book of verse, and with it became famous. This first work already bore the stamp of a free, revolutionary genius, a lover of progress, a hater of all opportunism, and one who felt deep in her heart the eternal unity of nature.

I met her directly after the war, when I visited my family in Paris for the first time since 1914. At this time, though forty years old, the Noailles looked much younger; she hardly seemed to be thirty. Though she had been ill ever since the birth of her only child, she always remained full of energy and love of life. She was greatly loved. She had given to those people who were near her much happiness and much pain, but always it was noble happiness and noble pain.

239

At our very first meeting we became friends. As so often was the case, at that time she was lying in bed, in great pain.

"I greet you most heartily, as an Austrian," were her first words. And she began to speak of Austria, where she had often lived. She spoke with a remarkable understanding of the old Austria, that had been so difficult to understand; and she showed a prophetic knowledge and foresight of the consequences the Treaty of St. Germain would bring to Austria, and to the whole of Europe. She was developing plans for Austria that were based on a real political insight. For this poet and dreamer was, when necessary, able to show the most logical and calculating intelligence. She was as wise and intelligent as only a great poet can be.

From this time on I often saw this true friend of my country. She helped me when I was worried about my country's fate. If poetry was the breath of her life, politics seemed to be the necessary food for her brain. She had devoted friends in all Cabinets of a Left nature. She often went to the League of Nations assemblies; and she had been present when Painlevé had made his great speech demanding the removal of Zimmermann from Austria. Afterwards she wrote me, "I am sure you are happy now. A great step towards Austria's future has been taken."

Another outstanding characteristic of this great woman was her courage, the courage that every really great spirit must have. She had the nature of a fighter. When Caillaux was imprisoned she plunged into the struggle for him, and wrote: "Never did Caillaux do anything against his country, not even in his thoughts. Whatever is said to his discredit must be a lie. Caillaux is innocent!" And fearlessly she stayed at his side right through the court case, sitting in the front of the court and demonstrating her belief in his innocence. In these moments this weak, tender creature was filled with an iron strength. But periods like these were followed by weeks of utter depression, in which she suffered indescribably. She had to take sleeping draughts, and to spend her days in darkness. When I called on her she would be lying in bed, her long black hair hanging down, her face deathly pale. Only her marvellous eyes seemed alive, with a burning intensity. Often she spoke so quickly and softly that one could scarcely follow her.

Only those who were lucky enough to have the opportunity of listening to the unequalled spiritual pyrotechnics of her conversation, could judge what this generous soul was lavishly giving away every hour and every day. Also she worked almost uninterruptedly, and in the rare intervals of her work she received Ministers, scientists, and leading journalists. She had an insight into the most secret political happenings. She was drawn into the discussion of scientific problems by those who were solving them, she wrote topical articles when she wanted to help someone or defend some cause.

Her salon was her bedroom. " The invention of sitting down," she said laughingly to me one day, " is one of the most disgusting mistakes of so-called progressive civilization."

Often on evenings when she was surrounded and besieged by people, her ladies' maid would come into the room bearing an evening frock. I remember one day the maid saying, " Madame la Comtesse has forgotten that she is dining with the President of the Republic."

Five minutes later she was standing up in full evening dress, a crown of flowers surmounting her beautiful head. " Such things shouldn't be taken seriously," she said. " I can't understand women who take hours to make themselves presentable. I know that it is only at the last moment that I can force myself to make any preparations to go out."

The Noailles was passionately absorbed in flying. Her interest began with Lindbergh's flight, when he first crossed the Atlantic. At this time Painlevé was War Minister. He invited Lindbergh to a *déjeuner* where Field-Marshal Foch and General Pétain were also present. We were sitting in the beautiful gardens of the War Ministry when Painlevé introduced Lindbergh to us. He was very young, very shy and very awkward. And when he met the Comtesse de Noailles he could not get a single word to pass his lips. But she began to speak in verse as if she was intoxicated, and improvised a poem—a copy of which I had but now seem to have lost. However, it was included in her complete works.

Such an unusual display of the imagination might seem to be an exaggeration. But it sprung from the amazing spiritual vitality that informed her and which, I am certain, shortened her life, which seemed to burn away in the fire of her genius.

She wanted to make a record of her life. Her last work had this aim. *Le livre de ma vie* was her title for an autobiography that reached far beyond the limits of a single life. It was a confession of all that was great, beautiful and tragic. Here could be found the rhythm of her life and her temperament, here the breath of lyricism was combined with the power of the intellect.

Another beautiful but melancholy day lives in my memory. It was in May 1929, at Versailles, when the election of the President of the Republic had taken place. Briand's election would have been the crowning of his whole life, which had been devoted to working in the cause of peace. The whole country wanted him to be President. The only force opposed to him was the reactionary majority of the Chamber under the leadership of Tardieu.

A political *déjeuner* took place at the Trianon Palace. Anne de Noailles was sitting with Caillaux. When I passed her she whispered into my ear : " The Right want to sabotage Briand's election. A tremendous intrigue is taking place. He must be warned."

The intrigue was completely successful. I will never forget the moment when the newly-elected President Doumer and the defeated Briand began their journey back to Paris. Thousands of people lined the roads, and there was not a single cheer at Doumer's passing. But when Briand appeared a storm of applause broke out.

We were standing quite close to him. With tears in her eyes the Comtesse de Noailles waved to Briand.

" His defeat is a defeat for world peace," she said to me. " This is a fatal hour for us and for Europe."

Never for a moment had this woman become a victim of war psychosis. She was *not* one of those mothers who did not know how to warn her sons from killing and being killed. To her son she dedicated one of the most impressive war songs ever written, " *Toi, dont la main n'a pas tué* . . ."—a song against the war.

She died when she was fifty-three, but she wanted to live on. " Ah, que vivre est divin," she sang, but also she sighed:

> " Mais moi qui dira mon délire
> Le jour que mon corps sera mort."

I can see her before me, as she was on the last occasion that I met her, in her bed, her beautiful, full lips, her eyes shining with an unworldly light. And I can hear her voice, the voice that had never broken with pain, the soft voice floating above her agony, carrying the music of her poetry with it. Poetry which, although it had been written many years earlier, was her last confession and her real good-bye.

> " Je vous laisse le clair soleil de mon visage
> Ses millions de rais
> Et mon cœur faible et doux eut tant de courage
> Pour ce qu'il désirait."

CHAPTER V

ALL the world's sympathies, all the courageous work of the Austrian people and its leaders, could not save the country from the effects of the terrible economic depression that began to ravage the whole world at the beginning of the 1930's. Solid economic structures, age-old institutions that had remained unshaken and practically untouched by the war, now began to crumble. No wonder that Austria, still suffering from post-war disorganization, could not withstand this storm. Once more she had to apply to the League of Nations, but this time with the better standing of a debtor who had proved worthy of a loan, because she had always kept her payments up to date.

In May 1932 a young man who had come from a peasant family became Bundeschancellor. His name was Engelbert Dollfuss. His home policy was to restore Austrian confidence in Austria, to keep her more and more independent of Germany. At this time his foreign policy was directed towards collaboration with France and England. Dollfuss was an economist, and he never stopped being one. To save the Tyrolean peasants from hunger—for as long as they were hungry they would constitute a rebellious element within the country—he had to find new markets for Austrian timber exports. It was a serious question : the Tyrolese unrest was taking the form of a desire for a union with Germany, where the growing National-Socialist party was preaching the gospel that the only thing necessary to banish cold and hunger was a magical formula of National Unity. In this vital question he hoped that France might help by taking some of the timber exports.

The French seemed ready to do this, but the negotiations

dragged on. Painlevé, true to his past record, wanted to help again. He had come to Vienna in September 1932, and greeted with admiration the courageous behaviour, the really Austrian optimism of our politicians. His serious illness during the winter prevented him from attending the French Chamber and Senate and pressing for the expediting of the timber agreement and the preparation of a new Austrian loan. But from his sick-room he did speak to his old friends and implore them to help.

I was with him when on January 29th, 1933, he received a telephone message that Adolf Hitler had become Reichs-Chancellor. For a moment or two he did not speak. Then, pale and moved, he said : " To-day, perhaps, will mark the death of European culture. And this in the twentieth century. . . . Poor, poor Austria. . . ." But he soon found his energies again, and up to the end he used them for the cause of Austria, which now was, as he said, " the last hope of everything admirable in German culture ". And how he admired it can best be seen, perhaps, from the manner of his death.

On June 28th, at seven in the evening, Painlevé asked for his secretary. As the latter told me afterwards, he was sitting in his arm-chair, fighting for breath. But he wanted to dictate —to dictate the undying words of Goethe whom he loved, in a new French translation. That he had chosen this writer, and just this part of his work to translate (without having the original German to hand), is significant.

" NUIT PROFONDE

Chant de Lyncæus (Gardien de la Tour)

> Né pour regarder
> Préposé pour contempler
> Consacré à la Tour
> Le monde me plaît.

Je regarde dans le lointain
Je vois de près
La lune et les étoiles
La forêt et les chevreuils
Ainsi je vois partout, l'éternelle beauté des choses
Et comme elle me plaît, je me plais ainsi moi-même.

Yeux! Yeux bienheureux!
Qui avez vu cela quoique cela ait pu être
C'était pourtant si beau."

Dr. Dollfuss, whom I had met at a reception at the French Embassy, rang me up in the autumn of 1933. He knew that I had a nursing home quite near Vienna but in the midst of beautiful and peaceful country, and he wanted some quiet place where he could remain incognito for three or four days. He asked me if he could come there for those days. Of course I was only too pleased to be of the slightest use to the man who, at that time, seemed to be the saviour of his country from the forces that were attempting to overthrow it.

So he came, worn out from fighting, but too preoccupied with his statesman's duties to pass the days without thinking and talking of the national and international situation. He said that it was his hope to get both economic and moral support from the Western democracies, to be able to consolidate the international situation, and thus make all the intrigues and propaganda of the German Nazi party impossible in Austria.

This was in the autumn of 1933. But when on February 12th, 1934, Dr. Dollfuss gave the order that unloosed rifle and machine-gun fire upon the Austrian working people, he must have lost all hope for the support of the Western democracies and have been compelled by Italy to carry out what cannot be called anything but an act of insanity—for it not only destroyed the necessary national unity that was required for defence against the foreign enemy—the Nazis; but also it made Austria lose her most valuable treasure—the sympathy of the world.

On Friday, March 11th, 1938, in the early afternoon, Egon Friedell, who was my best friend, called on me. He was one of the last living representatives of the type of Austrian who had flourished under the Hapsburg Monarchy. However much, and rightly, one condemns this monarchy, one thing about it cannot be denied—that at least under its régime a freedom of the kind that is necessary for the development of personality existed. Original people, uncommon individuals, geniuses, and creative minds, could develop.

One of the most prominent of these " anarchists of personality " who did not accept any convention was Egon Friedell, Doctor of Philosophy, author and actor. (Max Reinhardt loved him dearly, and it was of Friedell that he had said " No one can act better and more convincingly than a gifted dilettante ".)

Shortly after the war Egon Friedell had written a book that brought him international fame. His history of contemporary civilization is a work of profound philosophical insight, deep historical knowledge, and great artistic value. One thing in this book that I had disagreed with, even while he was writing it, was that Friedell was rather inclined to look to a dictatorship as being the solution of the problem of the ideal form of government. True, he meant a form of dictatorship similar to the ideal dictatorships of the ancient Greeks—enlightenment, goodness, and wisdom incarnated in the form of one man chosen by God for his qualities, his upbringing, and his love for the whole world. " A dictatorship without a gospel of hatred is impossible," I used to say to him. But he replied that only a man who did not know what hatred meant should become a dictator.

And so he was doubly unhappy when history made him realize his error—when Hitler became dictator of Germany;

Hitler, the man who had preached hatred all his life, nothing but hatred, hatred against the Jews, hatred against the French who had won the war, hatred against the British who had taken the colonies, hatred against the communists—incarnate hatred and revenge for imagined wrongs.

Friedell had always fought against Nazism, and he fought with redoubled energy when his own country seemed endangered by the spread of this foul plague. When he learned that Dr. Schuschnigg was to hold a plebiscite on Sunday, March 13th, 1938, he was filled with delight and happiness, since he was certain that Austria once and for all would show that she had remained true to herself, and would answer with an overwhelming YES to the question whether she wanted to remain politically and spiritually free.

Two days after it was announced that the Plebiscite was to be held, Egon Friedell and a few other friends assembled at my house for tea.

Our feverish hopes had created a state of semi-intoxication in us. All the time shouts of " Long live Schuschnigg " and " Long live free Austria " could be heard from the Rathausplatz and surrounding streets, making a background to our talk.

Oedoen von Horvath,[1] the young and brilliant writer of the book *Youth Without God*, which showed how the Germans during the process of what they call " making the youth fit " were killing their souls, came in rather late, and greeted us with the words " I'm late because it was difficult to get through the mass of people who are filling the streets. Not a single shout of ' Heil Hitler ' can be heard anywhere. The people are full of enthusiasm. I have spoken on the telephone with friends in the provinces too, and everywhere the same frenzied enthusiasm is to be found, since at last Schuschnigg has spoken the decisive and irrevocable words, ' Thus far and no farther.' We Austrians have found ourselves again. I am absolutely certain that the day

---

[1] Oedoen von Horvath has—after he had safely escaped the Nazis— been killed in the street in Paris, by a falling tree.

after to-morrow more than eighty per cent of the population will vote ' Yes.' "

" Certainly," said B——, the poet, who was always so well informed and so cautious. " Certainly. But Schuschnigg's words have had a dual effect. The Austrians now realize that they are no longer alone in facing the Nazi threat. They realize that Schuschnigg could not have taken such a decisive step without first having secured the help of the Western democracies. France and England, even Italy under their pressure, has certainly guaranteed that this plebiscite will take place undisturbed by any foreign intervention. And in just such a case as this Italy's promise is valuable, because of the three powers Italy is our only neighbour, and therefore in the case of any emergency can give immediate help."

" Mussolini's promises! " smiled Friedell sardonically. " If they are all that we have to rely on I'd better go home straight away, and get my luggage. You all know how I hate travelling —and because I know that the preparations for a journey are even more unpleasant than the journey itself, I always keep a suitcase ready packed with a few days' necessities. So that if I have to make a little trip I needn't take any trouble. Anyhow " (and here his jocular tone changed to deadly earnest), " in every sense of the word I'm ready for a journey at any time now."

A young journalist came in. He was so excited that he even forgot to make any greeting. " I have just come to let you know that we have received the best possible news from all parts of Austria. In the Tyrol the people are happy, cheering, a nightmare seems to have disappeared from the country. Those who had been threatened with terror up to yesterday, those who had demanded a plebiscite and despaired that their demands would not be listened to and that they might become martyrs for having made them—for them now there is nothing but happiness. The same is the case in the Vorarlberg. Only in Graz is there some excitement. The Nazis seem to have organized their main stronghold there, because they could not really get through to Vienna, and Graz is the strongest socialist fortress in Austria.

Many Nazi riots have broken out there, but the Socialists are strongly organized and they have come to an understanding with Schuschnigg, so Graz also is safe for us."

All this good news made me doubtful. It sounded too good to be true. In the later years of my life I had been called the Viennese Cassandra because of my caution and pessimism. So I interrupted his excited flow and said, " Don't you think that Hitler may try to do something to prevent this victory? Are you quite sure that this plebiscite will go off quietly and peacefully on Sunday morning? Don't you think it is possible that just because Austria and the Austrians have found themselves, just because this defeat would be so complete, Hitler might intervene —with threats of arms, or even with arms—to prevent this plebiscite taking place at all? "

All the short pause that followed my words was filled with the enthusiastic shouts from outside of " Heil Schuschnigg ", " Long live free Austria ", " We don't want the brownshirts ".

" Just listen to this," said Rudolf Beer, the famous theatrical producer, pointing to the window. " Could anyone dare to interfere amidst this enthusiasm? After all, even now there are plenty of foreigners in this town; the whole world has realized that Austria wants to remain Austria; and the powers, the League of Nations, the whole world, would protest if Nazi Germany tried to interfere. And the Nazis themselves would not be so foolish as to undertake such a dangerous task. Even if the Nazis took Vienna, they would always remain Austrian Nazis, and they would never be as cruel as the Prussians are. After all, Vienna is Vienna, and the same means cannot be used here as in Prussia. Haven't they got enough trouble already with the Southern Germans, the Bavarians and the Catholics? No, they can't be thinking seriously of ' an armed invasion of Austria '. The cost would be too great for them."

And with these optimistic words we said good-bye to each other. All of them were busy, all of them happy to be able to do whatever they could to increase the general enthusiasm and optimism.

I stayed at home. Already it was getting dark. In front of the house the voices had become quieter—probably because the crowd had gone on to some other part of the town, I thought. After having been actively connected with so many of my country's historical events I wanted to participate somehow in this great historical moment. I turned on the wireless. It was just past 7.30 on Friday, March 11th. I heard the well-known voice of Schuschnigg. He was in the middle of a speech, obviously propaganda for the plebiscite. . . .

" Before the whole world I declare that the reports issued concerning disorders created by the Austrian workers and the shedding of blood, the allegations that the situation had got out of the control of the Government were lies from beginning to end. . . ."

Perfectly true. I nodded in silent agreement. The voice continued after a short pause.

" President Miklas asks me to tell the people of Austria that we are not prepared to shed blood. We decided to order the troops to offer no serious—to offer no resistance. . . ."

What did it all mean? For a moment I was too agitated to listen. I only understood the last words:

" God protect Austria! "

I will never again see any of those friends with whom I had spent the last hours of the existence of a free Austria.

Egon Friedell committed suicide by jumping out of a window.

Rudolf Beer, who did not believe in the cruelty of Austrian Nazis, was attacked by a horde of Nazis and literally slaughtered. They tore out one of his eyes, broke several ribs, lacerated his chest, and he only escaped further torture by taking the poison that he had always carried with him since the Nazi danger had arisen.

My friend, Dr. Kunwald, who had been Seipel's right-hand man, also took poison to escape a worse death.

The young journalist who had spoken so optimistically and whose name I did not mention, is in the Dachau concentration camp, buried alive—already dead to me—for very few people ever emerge alive from that hell on earth.

With the help of my brother-in-law, Paul Clémenceau, and Paul Géraldy, and almost miraculous good luck, I succeeded in saving my grandson and myself. But the meaning had been taken out of my life, the life that was lived for Austria, the life of a woman who for fifty years had taken an almost daily part in the struggle for a country that was now no more. My life was empty, cut off from friends, home, and past.

Must I say : " Finis Austriae "?

No. I remember the strength of my friend Paul Painlevé, his undying love of humanity and his belief in its inherent goodness that persisted in the face of death. And I, too, will end with the words :

> " Ihr glücklichen Augen,
> Was je ihr gesehen
> Es sei wie es wolle
> Es war doch so schoen! "

INDEX